Dorian Lucas

SWISS DESIGN

BRAUN

122 Product Design

Preface

by Dorian Lucas

"The coat of arms of the federation is, within a red field, an upright white cross, whose [four] arms of equal length are a sixth longer than their width." (Federal decision of 12 December 1889 on the bearings of the coat of arms)

These few words not only define the Swiss national symbol but also describe one of the most successful design logos ever. The Swiss cross is not only a symbol of the country, but at the same time the memorable shape that is the epitome of the unadorned, functional and distinguished style of Swiss design. On December 12, 1889 the Swiss coat of arms was first decreed, followed by the mostly square Swiss flag. Variations of the Swiss cross have been recorded since the battle of Laupen in the year 1339, and it gained ground as the national symbol in various styles since the mid-15th to the mid-16th century. The corporate design of the federal administration, which took effect in 2007 defines the "Swiss Red" as the equivalent of Pantone 485, i.e. either 0/100/100/0 in CMYK, 255/0/0 in the RGB color scheme or as RAL 3020 traffic red. The ratio of the white cross to the red area is also not legally stipulated, but is defined in the corporate design as 6 for the cross area to 7 for the arms to 6 to outer flag edge.

Switzerland as a nation came into being in the 13th century, initially as a loosely organized confederacy. The Confoederatio Helvetica, as it is known in Latin (which is the basis for the country code CH), today consists of 26 cantons in which four languages are spoken - German, French, Italian, and Rhaeto-Romanic. Accordingly, the national identity is not based on language and culture. Rather, it is based on a sense of common history with a liberal, grass-roots democratic, and federalist tradition, along with the awareness that its four languages and political neutrality make it one of Europe's most unique nations. So unique in fact, that Switzerland remained a sole foreign nation surrounded by the open-bordered European Union.

With its approximately 7.8 million citizens, less people reside in Switzerland than in London. However, this limited number of citizens should by no means evoke the rural image of Heidi and her rustic grandfather of the children's tales by Johanna Spyri. A total of 5.7 million Swiss reside in urban settlements. The two books of the Swiss author were published in 1880/1881, when the urbanization of the country was just commencing. Today, agriculture only constitutes 1-2% of the gross national product, while the service industry and trade sector constitute 20% each, while the financial and real estate sector contribute around 10% each. The remainder belongs to the construction and insurance sectors. There are very few conglomerates in Switzerland, its economy is dominated by small and medium-sized companies, including many traditional artisan and high-tech firms. Clocks, machines and fabrics are the most important trades of the secondary sector. Tradition and high quality demands constitute the value-creating counterparts to high wages, which makes Swiss companies predestined for the production of exclusive items for global export to wealthy nations.

This inevitably requires good design - while there can be only one cheapest provider, there can be many best providers. Design as a factor for success is an integrated part of many Swiss products. By creating a high recognition value and highlighting the advantages of a product, design guarantees more stable sales and greater added value. The authorship of a specific designer can be as much a market value as the so-called “Swissness” of a product. This English-sounding catchword is used to attempt to market the association with Switzerland as an inherent quality of a product and to give it a trendy touch. It is frequently used in the context of products that incorporate the Swiss coat of arms and that have a similar purist design and occasionally even Calvinist functionality.

The question of the “right” design - whether trendy or timeless - emerged during the age of industrialization and culminated in 1907 in the establishment of the Swiss professional association. The first highlight of unadorned modern design was the work of the Swiss native Le Corbusier, who was, however, mainly active in France. The Bauhaus student Max Bill first posed the question of Swiss design at the special exhibition “Die gute Form” (the good shape) at the Basel samples fair in 1949. Answers included the starkness of “Swiss typography” of Josef Müller-Brockmann and his associates. Today, Swiss designers graduate from the École Cantonale d’Art de Lausanne or the Hochschule für Gestaltung in Zurich to work all over the world. Their creations by no means exhibit a single clearly defined style; rather they seem to be defined by a diversity of traditions and influences, as is characteristic of the whole Swiss nation.

Fashion Design

The Swiss world of fashion was born in 1916 when professional women, especially seamstresses in the large cities of Switzerland emerged established fashion sections. For example, the fashion establishments in the city of Aarau organized themselves into the Schweizerischer Frauengewerbeverband (SFGV - Swiss women's professions association). The charity organization arranged public fashion shows as part of its professional training and employment services during the economic crisis of the 1930s. Initially, the Swiss fashion sector was strongly influenced by international design trends. This was partially a result of the organized study trips of the SFGV and the emigration of later renowned Swiss fashion designers abroad. These include Robert Piguet (1901-1953) who moved to Paris at age 17, where he first worked for the French fashion designer Paul Poiret and the fashion label Redfern. In 1933 he established his own label and advanced in the following years to one of Switzerland's most successful designers. He even inspired later generations such as Christian Dior and Hubert de Givenchy. However, the international success of the Swiss fashion scene only took place much later. An important commercial center for this was the Textil & Mode Center Zurich, established in 1978. Since that time, Swiss fashion designers like Egon von Fürstenberg (1946-2004) exhibited their work together with and next to established Swiss brands such as Bally and Kandahar, while many young female designers currently receive attention with new labels. Whether “bare essentials,” dazzling surrealism or wearable everyday clothing - the scope of the Swiss fashion world is limitless.

Kandahar

The ski instructor and shoe maker Fritz von Allmen of Mürren was asked in 1932 to produce ski boots for the members of the local British Kandahar Ski Club. The result was so popular that the Ski Club offered the manufacturer the use of its name - marking the beginning of the classic winter boots series. Serial production of the typical design was launched in the 1930s and achieved international acclaim. In the late 1970s, Dieter von Allmen and his wife Konstanze assumed management of the company, successfully marketing the company's tested designs since that time. To this day, all products are manually produced.

Kandahar shoes are made of suede, cow or horse hide. Water-repellent upper leather and inner lining of breathable lambskin provide comfortable wear and protection from wet weather. The high-edged sole consists of several layers with warmth-insulation. A special rubber compound provides good friction even in snow and ice. This consistantly high quality is combined with constantly new designs. For example, recent models feature flamboyant colors such as the Alpina Pink, or animal hide looks, such as the Alpina Leopard and the Alpina Zebra.

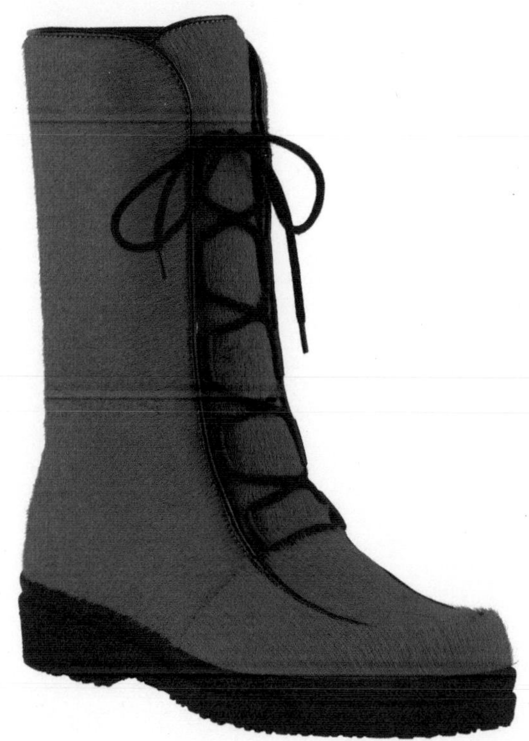

» When quality, functionality and good design meet it is frequently Swiss made. «

PHOTOS: COURTESY OF THE DESIGNER

» Creating the highest standards out of ordinary design «

Lela Scherrer

The collection of Spring/Summer 2010 includes 30 outfits in modern couture forms, made of classic couture materials like silk and cotton fabrics, cool wool and leather. Draped and constructed, folded tailoring pieces are contrasted by one-seam-cut jerseys and gift-bowed leather belts. The whole collection is held in pastel shades combined with strong color accents of reds, black, and white.

"Kleben Saegen Weben gegen den Ungeist", Autumn/Winter 2003/4, is a collection of 10 outfits, inspired by Schnitzler's "Anatol" 1910.
"The Alma Floor Lamp" was created by Lela Scherrer in cooperation with Christian Deuber and Jörg Boner. Made of cotton and wood, it constitutes a fusion project of fashion and interior design.

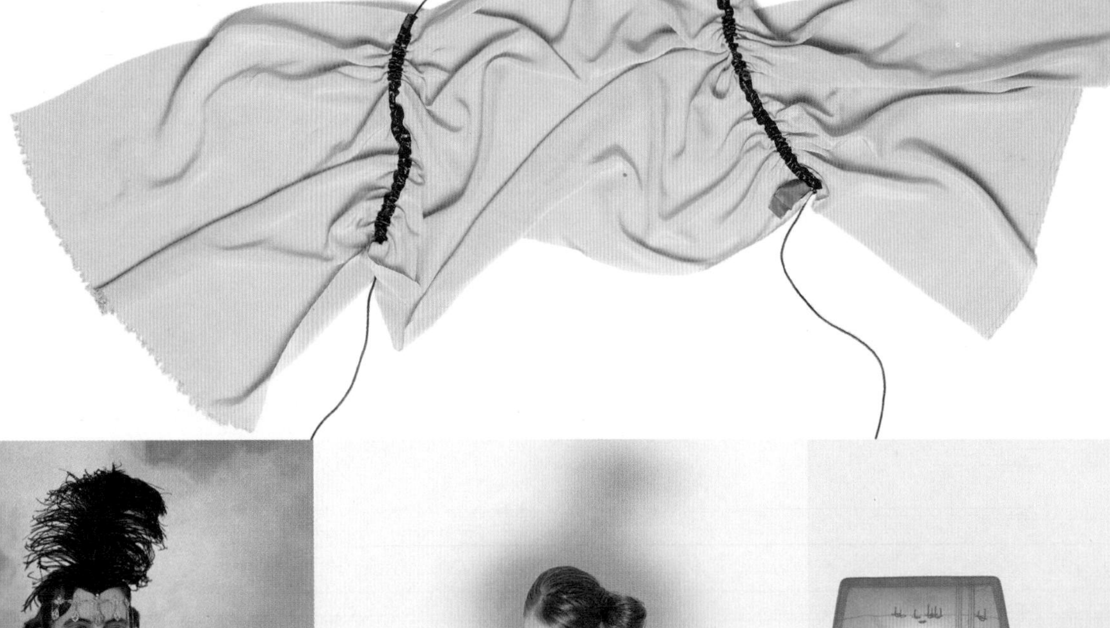

Fashion designer Lela Scherrer established her studios in Antwerp and Basel in 2002. Her work has always expressed a creative urge to integrate the diverse influences of her background: contemporary and traditional, local and foreign, handicraft and industrial elements have become her sources of inspiration. Combined with the technical knowledge of a tailor and her experience as a costume designer, various approaches fuse into her distinctive and versatile creative style. The studio seasonally launches a small womenswear collection, tailor-made exclusively for private customers and is working on fashion and concept design assignments for European fashion companies.

stéphanie baechler

The basic question expressed in the work of Stéphanie Baechler is to what degree our everyday life and our perception are shaped by the digital world and technology. For this reason, she consciously avoids digital components in her presentations. A very crucial role is played by the materials of her products, which she allows to guide her in the creative process. From heavy, woven materials to light fabrics, some enhanced by large-scale silk-screen printing or embroidered with delicate details, she adds a special touch, apparently far removed from the digitizer tablet.

Stéphanie Baechler is a fabric designer residing in St. Gallen. Following her graduation from HSLU Lucerne in 2008, she developed fabrics and products that received multiple awards. Her current work includes projects for Jakob Schläpfer of St. Gallen.

» A textile implementation and interpretation concerning human beings, bodies and computers – deliberately foregoing the presentation of digital esthetics. «

PHOTOS: SUSI LINDIG; DANIEL TISCHLER AND ANDRI STALDER

Catherine Dubler

» Translating artisanship into contemporary design «

This fully handcrafted collection is a form of minimal leather couture and generates a fresh vision in menswear. To realise the studio-based technique, all the pieces are made of lamb nappa leather.

One of the key objects is the "Golden Rope Shirt". By playing with proportions, the gilded "rope chain" becomes the central feature of the design, giving an abstract look to a simple leather T-shirt. The boxing gloves are not, as could be presumed, mere accessories, but one of the key elements of the collection. Entrapment procedures create delicate structures on the surface of the jacket.

Catherine Dubler's work is influenced by traditional artisanship based on her tailoring background, which she translates into innovative contemporary design through new processing methods. Affected by her study abroad, her unconventional design style is distinguished by an open approach to men's fashion. Her work features a strong conceptual foundation and intensive research of possible implementation methods. At the same time it exhibits her love and commitment to details coupled with high quality finishes.

PHOTOS: NICOLAS VENTOURAKIS

Anita Moser

This women's collections are distinguished by her surprising choice of themes and their implementation in innovative design solutions. They combine industrial manufacturing with handcrafted details. The draped "Peep toe ankle boots" from the winter collection or the pumps with braided details from the summer collection are good examples of this approach. Practically a classic, the sandals with a shaped leather sole and knotted acrylic rope are another example. The carefully crafted yet sturdy ankle boots of the men's collection are long-lived and independent of seasons. The collection contains timeless designer pieces that are complemented by new models every year. All designs will remain available for many years.

» Beautiful shoes are beautiful shoes are beautiful shoes. «

Anita Moser has been designing women's shoes since 2003 and men's shoes since 2009, under the "Anita Moser" label in Basel. The collections stand for unique women's shoes that are nevertheless suitable for everyday use, as well as new interpretations of classic male shoes. The collections are distinguished by the surprising choice of themes and their implementation in innovative design solutions. The shoes combine industrial manufacturing with handcrafted details and unique items are serially produced. The shoes have been sold in Japan, China and Europe since the year 2003.

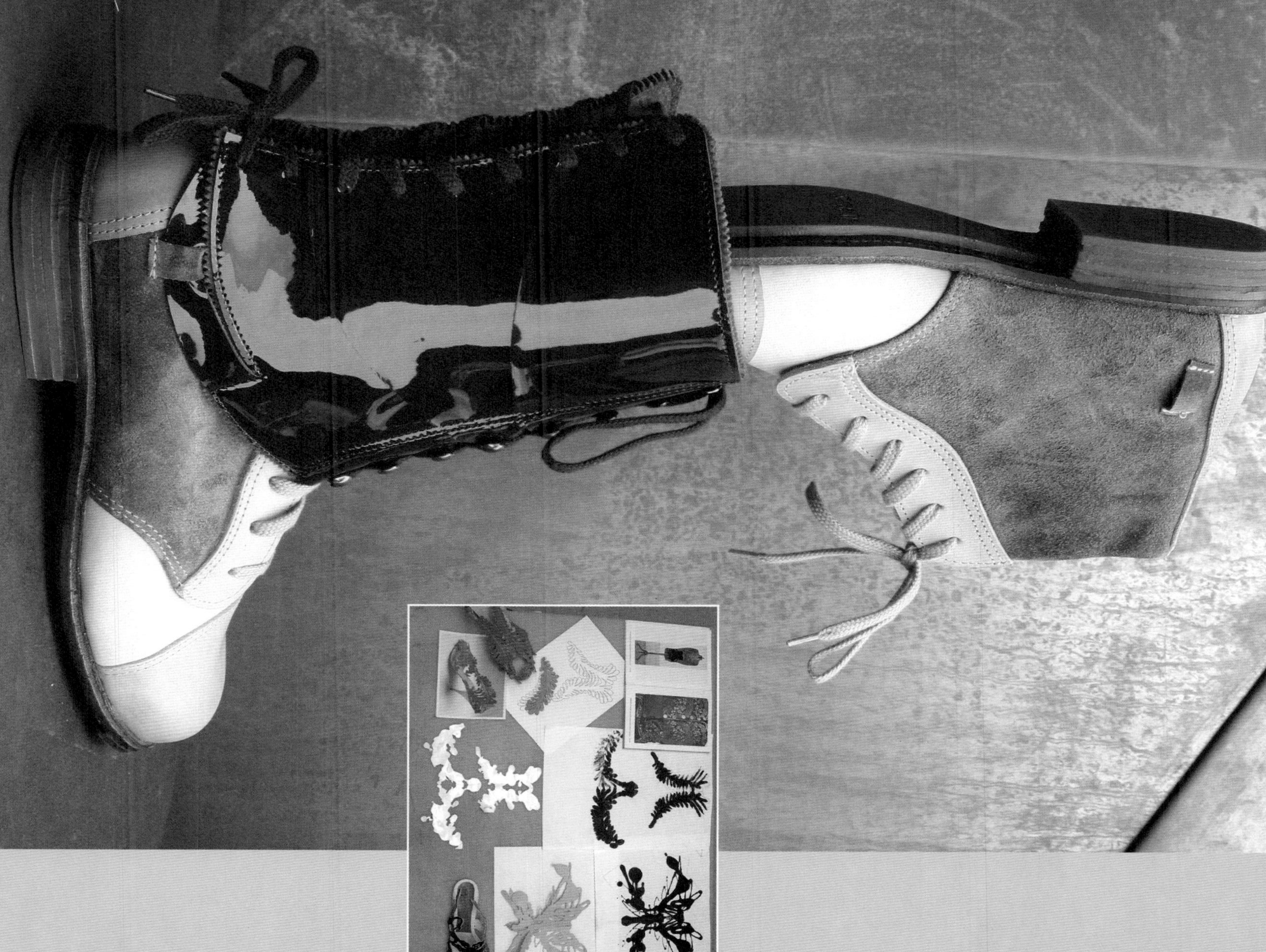

PHOTOS: COURTESY OF THE DESIGNER

Claudia Güdel

The Basel-based fashion designer Claudia Güdel emphasizes the functional honesty of her creations. Each seam has a purpose and the interior of every individual design is so lovingly crafted that it is worn with pride. Claudia Güdel combines high-performance materials with pleasant natural fibers for the busy everyday lives of men and women. The principal item of her collection is the “Ninja Top”, a high-necked hooded jacket made of Schoeller Textil fabric with integrated gloves. Variations of it include functional SoftShell coats and dresses made of wash-and-wear DrySkin quality. Claudia Güdel's collections are exclusively produced in Europe and Switzerland.

The men's wear label “Claudia Güdel” was established in the year 2002 by the designer. Since 2004, the label's headquarters are at Markgräflerstrasse 34 in Basel. At these generous facilities, fashion is developed, produced and presented. In 2007, Claudia Güdel won the National Swiss Design Award. In the winter of 2008, she launched her first women's collection and opened the first Claudia Güdel women's/men's wear store at Bäckerstrasse 56 in Zurich. Claudia Güdel's women's/men's wear are also sold at stores in Basel, Zurich and Vienna as well as through her own website.

PHOTOS: MARK NIEDERMANN, BASEL

» Black Sculptures «

roecke.ch

The series “Glück” (luck) promises its wearers luck at their side. All lucky skirts have two color-coordinated, slim lucky bands sewed to the waist, which function as talismans and accompany the wearer throughout her day. “Gently moved” shows that life is always in motion, even when it seems to stand still. The same applies to this collection. A slight disharmony between the exterior and interior fabric results in a new arrangement of the folds with every move. In “Shifting faces” different colored appliqués are slightly shifted, resulting in colored areas and interims. The cut edges with short fringes soften the austere lines and interrupt the precise shapes.

The office of Michèle Kägi focuses on one-of-a-kind distinguished skirts. Select materials, clear and feminine silhouettes, and subtle grace combine to create a sensual touch. The fabrics are conceived in-house and manually silk screen printed on cotton. The noble silk and modern wool are also top quality. Each series elaborates the content and look of a conceptual idea,

» What people wear tells a great deal about their qualities. «

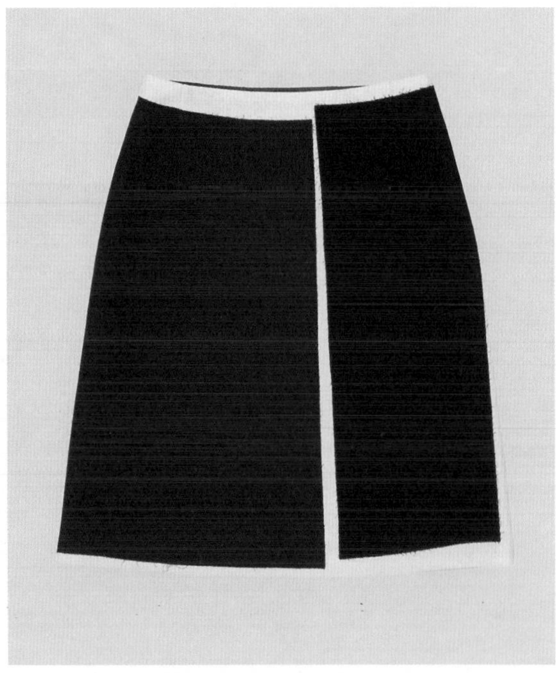

and each model is given its own identity through its name. Accessories and price tag reflect the concept of the series, in turn integrating every individual object into the overall context of the work.

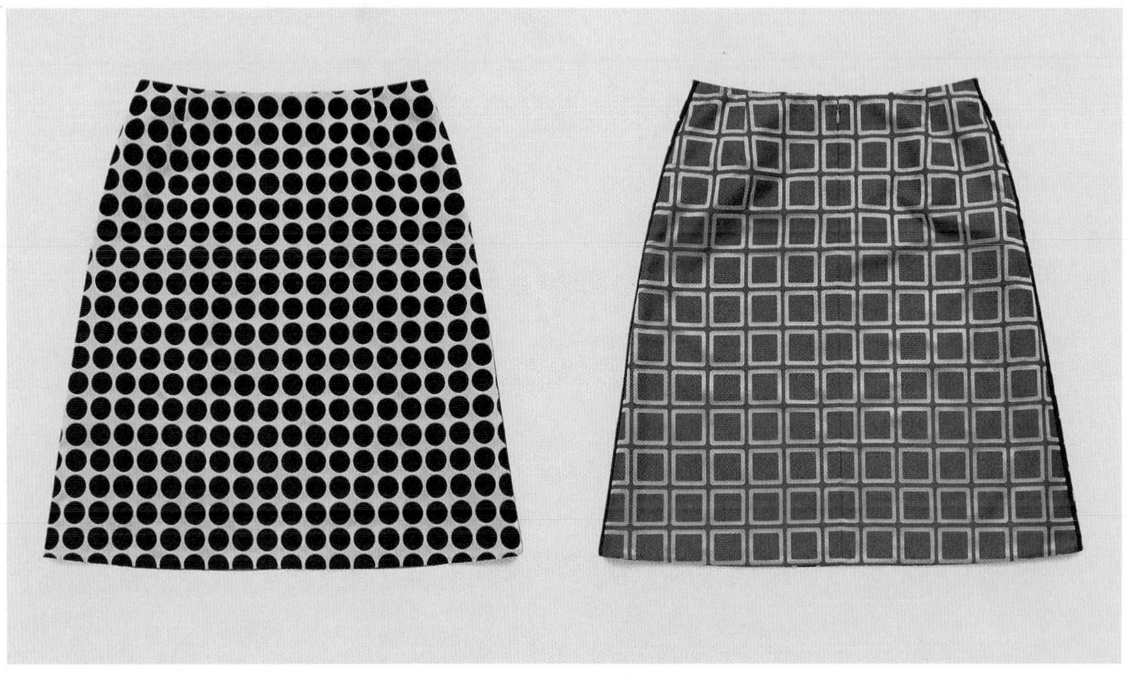

PHOTOS: COURTESY OF THE DESIGNER

Beige

The spring/summer collection 2010 by Beige is entitled "Magnolia". The clothes have compelling asymmetrical cuts, sophisticated patterns, and expressive colors. Pixel-style digital print patterns and intersecting squares are found throughout the collection. The skirts have slim silhouettes, while the collars of the dresses and sweaters have very playful details. The collection includes the sweater "Red Kiss" in coral red/orange, the printed skirt "Daiquiri" in anthracite/coral red/orange, the printed dress "Sky" in steel blue/black and the printed top "Sky" in black/sky blue.

Beige is the label of fabric designers Manuela Helg and Karin Maurer. Since establishing the label in 1996, the designers use established and new textile methods to develop unconventional fabric and knit designs. Every collection is seen as a portion of an ongoing creative interaction. The result is a series of self-confident and wearable clothes and accessories that are timeless and yet in line with an uncompromising contemporary spirit. Since 2001, the designers have been presenting their collections at their own salesroom in Zurich. The products are manufactured in Switzerland in small quantities.

» The universe is not green. It is beige. «
Tages-Anzeiger, 09.03.2002

PHOTOS: DANIEL SUTTER / BEIGE

Bally

Bally, the brand that is synonymous with luxury and elegance, was established in Switzerland in 1851. It is famous for its shoes and accessories as well as Prêt-à-porter fashion, which combines elegant style, high craftsmanship, and the best materials into a casual elegance. In 1851, Carl Franz Bally in Schönenwerd initially established an elastic ribbon and suspender factory, but within the same decade, shoes became the main line of business. In the late 19th century, the company began its global expansion course that continues to this day. The product line, Scribe, by Max Bally, grandson of the founder, became a core element of the collection in the 1950s. Brian Atwood was appointed creative director of the company in 2007.

Bally products are distinguished by the use of precious materials and fine leather for models that reflect the company's heritage and offer luxurious functionality with exquisite craftsmanship in a modern form. The design is clearly northern European, with deliberately masculine and feminine styles. The in-house archive contains 13,000 models, which are a key source of inspiration for product development. One characteristic of Bally is the red and white so-called "train-spotting" strip, which is frequently repeated. The latest offer from the brand includes a "made to order" line, which allows customers to select the material, design and color of the shoes with gilded silver soles, embossed silver emblems and personalized names, written on the shoes' lining.

» Elegance, Quality and Craftsmanship. «

PHOTOS: BALLY

Caroline Flueler

In her creative work, Caroline Flueler specializes in the design of accessories and cover fabrics. The collection "Aberdeen" features her work in the area of fashion accessories and includes a tie and socks in lively, yet unobtrusive colors and patterns. The home accessory collection "Boston" consists of plaids, pillows and hot-water bottles that add style and comfort to the home. For the rather more public domain of Swiss International Airlines, Caroline Flueler created the design, concept and color scheme for the seat covers and cabin furnishings. In addition, she developed the foulards and ties for the cabin crew.

» Simple & clear patterns are a result of complex work. «

Caroline Flueler established her one-woman enterprise in 1994, where she initially created her own fabric designs in the areas of home furnishings and fashion. Parallel to the exclusive collections, which she expands successively, she set up a second line of business with design projects for well-known companies (Tisca Tiara, Bernhardt Design NY, Lucerne Festival, etc.) Design expert Tyler Brûlé hired her in 2002 for the branding of the new «Swiss International Air Lines». Since then, she has worked as a consultant and designer in charge of the textile cabin furnishings of the airlines.

PHOTOS: COURTESY OF THE DESIGNER AND SWISS INT. AIR LINES

Christa Michel Knitwear

The Michael Jackson sweater was produced in a limited series of five. The work with the knitting machine was based on a figurative approach. The costumes for the Electro Pop band Taxi val Mentek were created in close cooperation with Christoph Hefti. The design of full-body costumes and the artistic details turned the clothes into objects of art. The pareo, on the other hand has a multifunctional character. It can be worn as a skirt, a warming wrap or a simple woolen blanket. This way it fulfills the much-propagated renewed longing for domesticity while commenting on the cocooning trend.

» Individual knitwear, charming & warming. «

PHOTOS: SHIRANA SHAHBAZI, CAT TUONG NGUYEN, TAXI VAL MENTEK

The sole proprietorship Christa Michel Knitwear was established in 1998 as a knitting manufacturer. On the one hand, it is a research laboratory and competency center for specific techniques of computer-assisted hand knitting machines. On the other hand, it is a production site for individual and limited series of a varied range of design, fashion and accessory products. The graduated fabric designer manufactures some products herself at her own studio in Zurich and works with selected production manufactures in Switzerland and Europe.

Alltag Agentur

» THIS IS REALLY GRAND CINEMA «

SonntagsZeitung Schweiz, 14.September 2008

The fashion collection Sentis is a culturally motivated product. It combines young design with traditional craftsmanship to create contemporary everyday clothing. The products are exclusively developed and produced in the eastern Swiss regions of St. Gallen and Appenzellerland. The innovative fabrics project aims to carry on with the century-old textile craftsmanship tradition and to create a new fashion label. The designs by Sentis are inspired by traditional costumes and can thus act as identity-creating items of clothing.

Everyday culture denotes the significance of habits and objects of everyday life. The significance of an object depends on the consumer. Creating significance is therefore a key objective of the communication of company and product concepts. Founded in the year 2005, the Alltag agency considers its core objective to be the shaping of the perception of a product or an institution in everyday life.

PHOTOS: IMAGE FOTOGRAFIE: CLAUDIA KNÖPFEL + STEFAN INDLEKOFER
LOOK BOOK FOTOGRAFIE: NICOLAS DUC

Inés Bader Textildesign

These products from the studio of Inés Bader are valued by designers and architects. They occupy a niche market in high-quality furnishings, accessories and jewelry stores, museum shops and fashion boutiques. The machine-knitted neck scarf “Tartaruga” was developed in 1997 and became the trademark of the studio and a Swiss design classic. The neck scarf “Luna” is made of a delicate silk fabric, which is exclusively tailor-made and conceptualized by the designer. It is rolled all around and, similar to the knitted scarves, it is seamless. The business socks with the colored tips are designed on the foot and also cut a good figure outside the shoe.

» Don’t call me a fashion designer, rather call me a thread acrobat, a thread conductor or a fabric composer. «

The designer Inés Bader describes herself as a color-addicted, yarn acrobat. Her specialization is the construction of fabrics from colored yarns, i.e. the development of knitted fabrics or cloth and not their use in manufacturing. The fabrics are developed and perfected directly on the loom or the knitting machine. Dimensional constructs can only emerge from the interaction with materials and techniques. High-tech computer programs help control the machines. She considers neck scarves to be the perfect manifestation of fabrics - they have no front and back, but only two fronts.

PHOTOS: COURTESY OF THE DESIGNER

Elif Gedik

"Marais Girl" – inspired by the Marais district in Paris, this feminine collection wants to convey to its customers a touch of Parisian "chic." The items are esthetic and pragmatic at the same time. Designer Elif Gedik allows the reflections of her imagination to guide her. She uses mixed materials to create ingenious pieces of clothing that are equipped with a practical zipper in the back. The aim of her collection is to develop each individual item of clothing to make it wearable and suitable for everyday use.

» Fashion is in the sky. «

Stylist Elif Gedik has been working independently since the year 2008 under the name Marais Girl. Her studio is located in Aarberg. Marais Girl translates Parisian chic into Swiss application. Esthetics and pragmatism always form a single entity in her collections, thus transforming the latest fashion trends into comfortably wearable forms.

PHOTOS: COURTESY OF THE DESIGNER

Furniture Design

Closely connected to traditional craftsmanship, Swiss furniture design in its modern form emerged in the 1930s through companies such Wohnbedarf. The close cooperation with renowned architects and artists resulted in classic furniture items such as the adjustable chaise-longue LC4 by Le Corbusier (1887-1965), Pierre Jeanneret and Charlotte Perriand. In the following decades, Switzerland achieved international acclaim with many companies such as Thut Möbel, Theo Jakob and the Röthlisberger Schweiz collection. In addition to Le Corbusier, Switzerland's most famous furniture designers include the Swiss architect, artist and designer Max Bill (1908-1994). However, both he and Le Corbusier did not create their best-known pieces of furniture in Switzerland. For example, in 1954 Max Bill in cooperation with Hans Gugelot created the Ulmer Hocker (Ulm stool) for the Hochschule für Gestaltung in Ulm, the most prominent design institution of the German speaking world after World War II. At this time, this stool served as a seat, side table, speaker's podium, shelf, and tray for students. It still fulfills this purpose today, but has advanced into a costly symbolic classic item. This is because designer furniture has long since ceased to be merely functional, but is instead an expression of individuality while constituting pieces of art in their own right. Sometimes simple and elegant, and sometimes playful and provocative, the furniture is present at the workplace, the home and in public areas. The continuous introduction of new materials and shapes increases the esthetic value of the furniture, accommodating not only changing fashions, but also individual preferences and characters, while being in harmony or deliberate disharmony with the surroundings. At the same time, it reflects the technical advances of their eras and highlights the mastering and limitations of specific methods.

Studio Hannes Wettstein

The NOMOS watch "Zurich" combines the best of Glashütte, Germany and Switzerland. The clockwork is manufactured in Saxony, Germany and encased in the best Swiss design. Large but not dangerous, noticeable but far from pretentious, Zurich is a watch that remains modest despite all its size.
"Delphi" is a new modular couch concept consisting of eleven different modules that allow many possible individual and unique sofa solutions. The collection "Patio" consists of a chair and an arm chair, adding a new touch to a classic element such as honeycomb weaving, expressing a balanced and clever mix of technology, handicraft and tradition.

Studio Hannes Wettstein researches, develops and implements furniture, objects of daily use and interior spaces for national and international clients. The sector most often associated with the name Hannes Wettstein is undoubtedly furniture and product design. For many years, the studio has been developing all types of objects for well-known companies. The focus of the studio's work is on understanding the nature and the context of a product, a space, or a piece of furniture and to get it into the appropriate shape by the right means. The agency was founded in 1991 by star designer Hannes Wettstein.

» Finding distinctive archetypal solutions «

PHOTOS: COURTESY OF THE DESIGNER

Frédéric Dedelley

The Evolution Chair was developed for Burri Public Elements AG in 2002 and is a street furniture object made of stainless steel. It is a pivoting stool for urban spaces, combining functionality with a minimalist design. The Haiku wardrobe was developed more for private than public areas for Lehni AG 2004. It is made of aluminum and displays a significantly clear geometry with plane surfaces. Its design language is cool and modern and its Physique is large, Roomy and lightweight. the upholstered armchair Wogg 47 for wogg AG, is reminiscent of Danish style furniture of the 1950s translated into a modern form. The framework with its light and clear structure contrasts with the plump and comfortable cushion. Corner, a hybrid accessory combining a tray with a mirror has been designed for Studio Domo.

» I question the features and origins of existing typologies in order to renew them. «

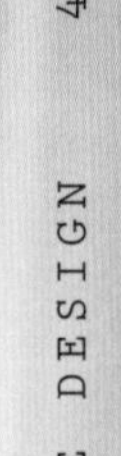

Frédéric Dedelley conceives objects, furniture, exhibitions and interiors for swiss and international clients. His projects often combine simplicity and functionality with a sense of playful irony. One of his central concerns is to question the features of existing typologies in order to redefine them. In addition to familiar design strategies such as research, analysis and the specifications of commissioned work, he frequently uses his collected photographs of unexpected situations or curious objects as an inspiration and as a starting point of the design process.

PHOTOS: EVOLUTION: HEINRICH HELFENSTEIN; HAIKU: CHRISTIAN KURZ; WOGG 47: MILO KELLER; CORNER: STUDIO DOMO

Stilo

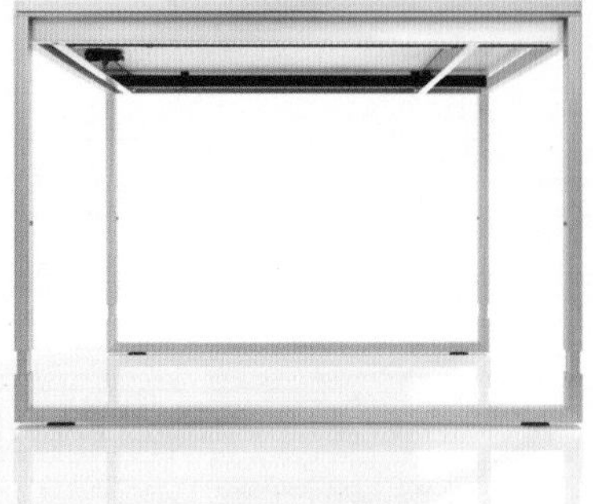

Stilo began in 1954 with selling electronic calculators and launched its own office furniture series ten years later. Since the establishment of the Stilo AG company and the move of its headquarters to the Appenzellerland region, the company has experienced constant and continuous growth. From the start, the company applied an innovative corporate concept with slim, agile structures. This way, Stilo AG was able to establish itself as a leading Swiss company in the office furniture sector and to react flexibly to the needs of the market.

L.One is a table that adjusts to its user. With its individual design it can be used from the back office to top managerial levels. It is simple, yet elegant design, the table height can be adjusted without tools and allows working while standing up or seated.

Face is a shelf cabinet system with individual elements that can be combined into an unlimited number of modules. The front and reverse sides are identical, allowing it to also look good when free standing, while the modules can also be arranged alternately. Face does not require handles and can be opened by a slight pressure on the front.

» More timeless, elegant, functional ... practically perfect! «

PHOTOS: STILO AG

greutmann bolzern designstudio

The work of this successful team is distinguished by clear shapes and materials. This design office's key area of operation is the world of offices from room dividers to lamps to entire corporate identities. This topic is particularly important to the team since it involves the decoration of rooms, creating a link to architecture. The studio's work has received many awards. Since 2003, Carmen and Urs Greutmann jointly hold a professorship for product design at the Academy of Fine Arts in Munich.

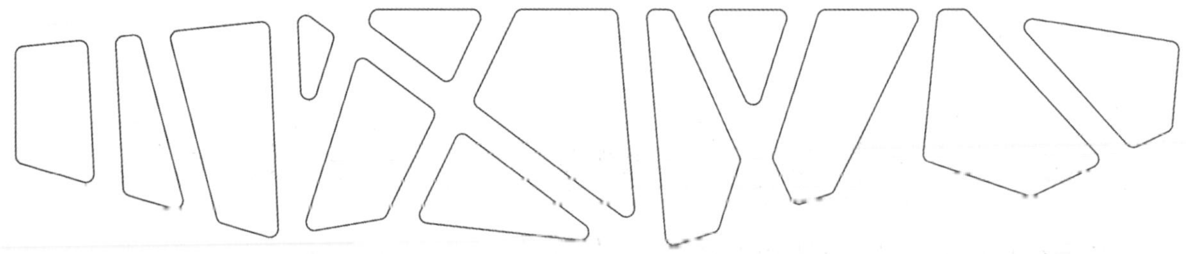

When entering the First Class check-in at Zurich airport, visitors are received by an elegant and quiet ambiance. Unique reception tables, inspired by the shape of a rotary engine, provide an exclusive welcome.

For the booth of Lista Office at the Designers´ Saturday in Langenthal 2008, three kilometers of strip were threaded into aluminum strips on top and on the bottom. This results in curved room dividers with great esthetic appeal.

» Design happens when head and hand are in sync. «

PHOTOS: COURTESY OF THE DESIGNER

Thut Möbel

Marketed internationally under the brand name «Thut Möbel», this furniture collection is distinguished by its cleverly conceived and innovatively functional models. In a specific market niche, «Thut Möbel» addresses a customer segment that values quality, attention to technical details, and esthetics. Whether tables, shelves or closets, the design of "Thut Möbel" is always simple, modern and attractive. Functionality and innovation are always the basic premise and content of the products, all of which are designed and produced in-house.

» The idea (invention) is the basis of a product (no sensationalism). «

Walter Thut established his carpentry workshop in the Swiss city of Möriken in 1929. His son Kurt Thut radically changed the product range starting in 1953, as he designed new products after graduating from the Kunstgewerbeschule in Zurich. In 1958 the carpentry work shop was complemented by a new manufacturing hall planned by Kurt Thut who established the Thut AG in 1970 after taking over the firm. Today, he manages the company with a staff of 12 together with his sons Benjamin (an industrial design graduate) and Daniel (an airplane mechanics graduate).

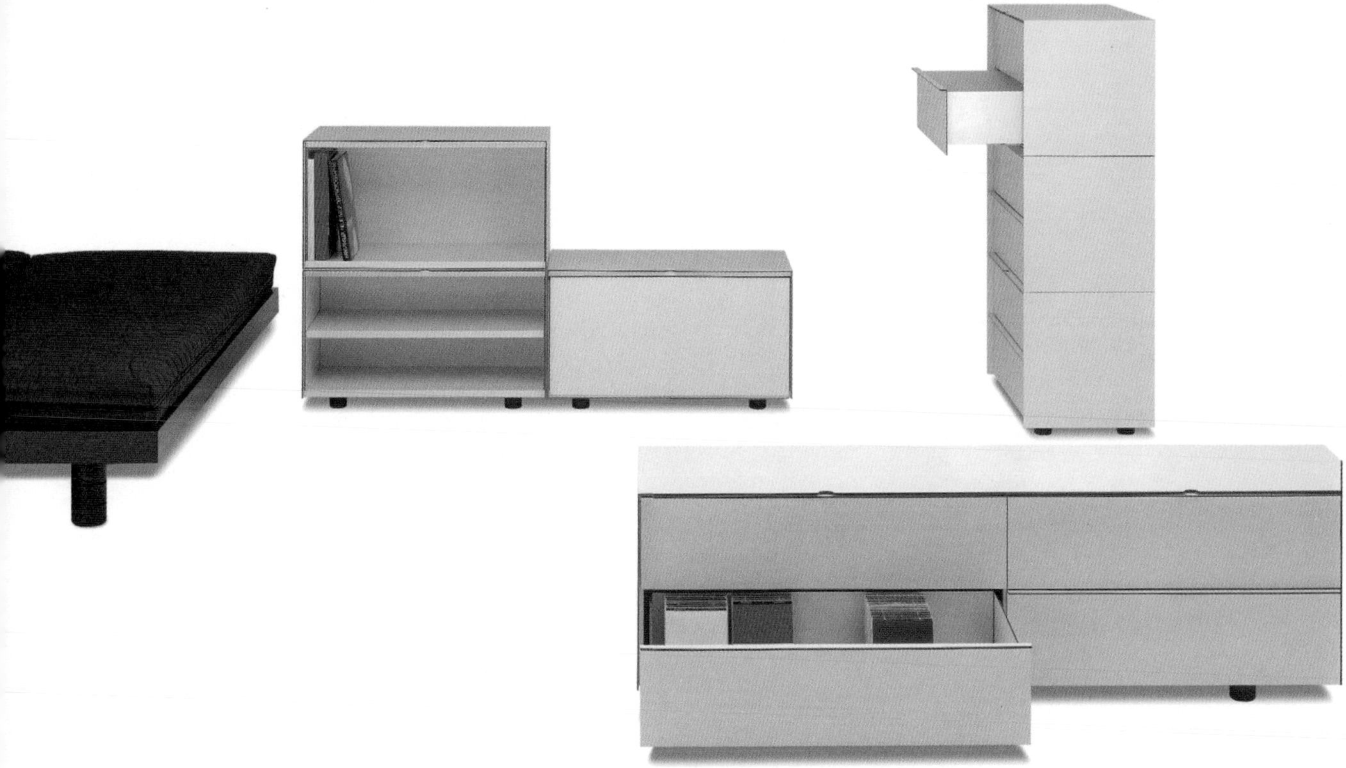

PHOTOS: COURTESY OF THE DESIGNER

Ramon Zangger Möbelwerkstatt

In the designs for the table "il tavolin", sideboard "la zaisa", and cabinet "modulor" the aim was to reinterpret alpine furniture styles without rustic elements. The aim was not to deny the place of origin and maintain high recognition values, while working with regional resources.
The design of the cabinets "spler" and "schatulla" focused mainly on reinterpreting traditional ornaments with contemporary finishing methods and to apply old rosette patterns to furniture and built-in components.
The interior design of the mineral spa "Samedan" has alpine decorations on surfaces that are both drilled and milled. These consist either of picture scenes or repetitive ornamental bands.

The R. Zangger-Rechsteiner furniture manufacturer operates like a handicraft workshop; there is no design office, only raw materials, machines and work benches. Its work is seen as a counterbalance to the increased gaudiness of the regional identity. With passion and dedication, exemplary furniture is created that allows a contemporary interpretation of the alpine region with simple local resources without resorting to kitsch. The objects are authentic and proudly evolved from the region - "in möd dal lö" (touched by the location)

PHOTOS: REMO NAEGELI AND STEFAN ROHNER

Christophe Marchand Design

"Aurea" has an attractive simple and cubic design coupled with high-quality finishing. Its esthetic appeal cleverly disguises its technical intricacies. For example, if required, a functional pillow supports an upright seating position in which one can easily write, read or work on the PC.
At first glance, the easy chair "Marvin" has an astonishing perfectly shaped seat bucket, which differs optically from conventionally designed furniture. The attractive exterior is very elegant and promises comfort.
The technical construction of the "Wogg 52" consists of only 5.6 millimeter-thick slim composite board whose delicate appearance is further enhanced by the white surface area.

The Atelier Marchand is a center of creativity. Visiting the studio in the brightly lit factory halls of the venerable Maag company offers a one-of-a-kind experience. On location, visitors can admire a very special furniture showroom, gain an exclusive insight behind the scenes of contemporary design, and receive valuable information from a personal talk with the designers. The synthesis of innovative design processes and stylish furniture presentation guarantees unique impressions, incorporating powerful designs, daily life and functionality.

» The simplicity of the beginning is an illusion that is shattered as soon as the peripheral problems become sufficiently clear. The simplicity of the end usually consists of a hard-earned result and a stroke of luck. «

PHOTOS: COURTESY OF THE DESIGNER

Heinz Julen

Different lines of work converge in the offices of Heinz Julen. In the year 2001, he established the company ARS MAROBAA AG (Nepalese for “My father”), which today has eleven employees. This branch of the operation is responsible for the production of furniture and lamps and is also active in the creation of the various buildings by the artist. Another branch is the architectural firm Heinz Julen Idee, in where two architects are in charge of project planning and concepts.

This block-shaped loft was built in 2002. It measures 300 square meters and is accessible via an elevator or a steep access above the roofs. The completely glazed side facing the valley, as well as two bedrooms, that are only partitioned off by glass panels, offer a generous view of the outside. Inside, the loft features a four-meter-long glass table that is illuminated at night, and can be suspended from the ceiling and electrically raised. Each object was custom-made for the project. Materials were kept as natural as possible and combined with modern shapes.

» Maintaining the characteristics of materials «

PHOTOS: COURTESY OF THE DESIGNER

jpbd

"Modular Racks Staple" is a shelf system inspired by scaffolding, requiring no nails, screws or glue. The structure is stabilized by metal clamps, and stability is further enhanced by its combination of oak wood, colored plexiglass panels and steel hooks. The basic models offer multiple combinations and the shelf system can be put together, taken apart and rebuilt at will. "Geometric" is a mirror and tree side table playing with the same assembly concept.

Jean-Philippe Bonzon has created a wide range of products during the past few years, including his boot removal device, a hair slide with bristles, and lamps made of cable binders. His objects stand out because of the choice and use of materials as well as his functional solutions with their tongue-in-cheek humor. Today he works as a product designer in different structures, cooperating in China with the architecture firme nhdro, and in Switzerland with the collective Daredo and with the architecture office aabe based in Ecublens.

» Home swiss home «

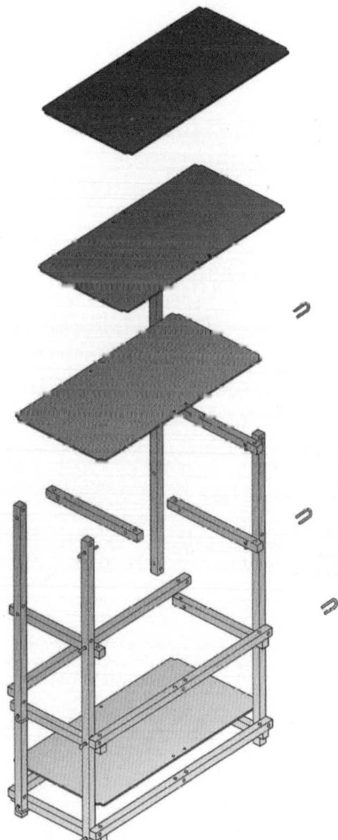

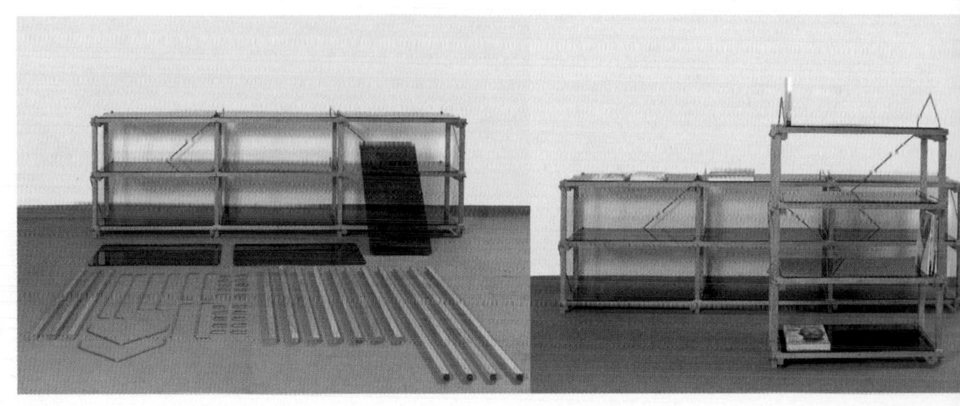

"Bricolo Chair" is designed for children. This chair is inspired by the traditional wood and plastic "shape fitting" for children. Assembling becomes a game and children become craftsmen or new designers. Each chair is sold in a flat package.

PHOTOS: JPBD

Rovero Adrien Studio

"Flip" is based on a simple set-up: a board and two trestles. This type of improvised writing table has a very clear characterization and a simple principle with no particular mechanism. Anodized and implemented in aluminum, the "pimp" stool and low table are based on a simple construction principle: a standard H profile and a folded sheet that become the connecting elements. Anodizing gives it a particular shiny look, which completes the simplicity of the construction.
The object "Potique" defines a space for reading and provides good lighting. It allows the reader to put his/her favorite seat underneath. The feet support a red lighting box that is usually suspended from the ceiling.

» Design as a meeting point «

Rovero Adrien Studio was founded in the year 2006. The studio's works were already exhibited in many European countries and its regular customers include a number of international design companies like Droog Design (NL), Dim (D) and Campeggi (IT). The work is based on a precise observation of elementary needs, where everything is the basis of speculation, hypotheses and imagination. With powerful details, he combines practical use as well as commonplace and extraordinary elements, providing unexpected simple and relevant solutions.

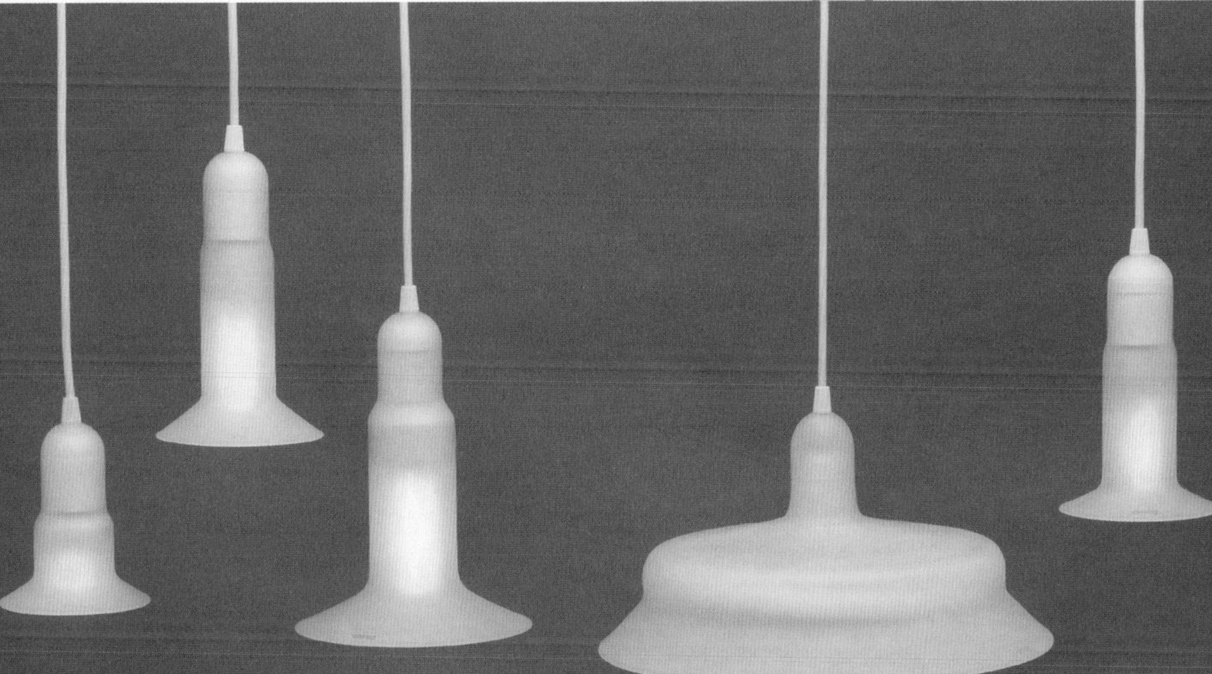

PHOTOS: OLIVIER PASQUAL

d'Esposito & Gaillard

The products of d'Esposito & Gaillard are distinguished by simple esthetics with clearly expressed shapes. At the same time, each product has a special characteristic that distinguishes it from the other models in its category. For example, the floor lamp "Detour" has a simple and elegant form, the special gimmick being the detour of the supportive rod around the switch, which breaks up the straightness of the model. The office table "Apendix", however, features a diagonal bar that is the simple solution to two problems at once. Despite the use of monitors, colleagues can establish eye contact without requiring a space-consuming angled table construction.

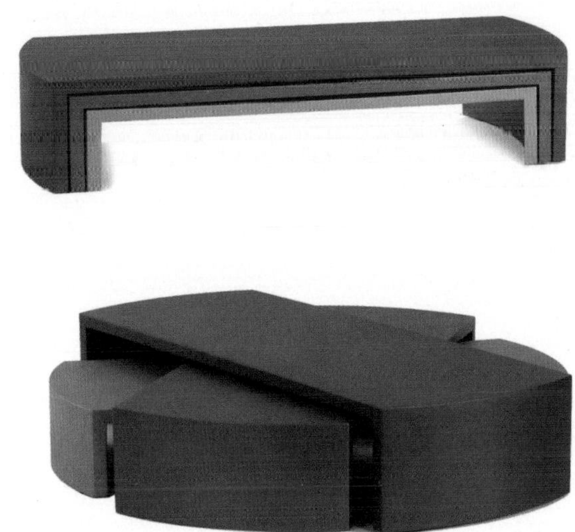

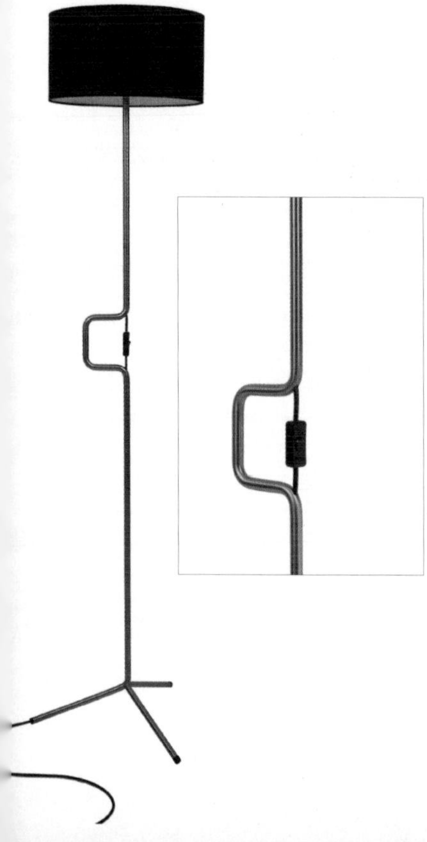

» Poetry helps function work. «

PHOTOS: NEWEBA AG (LAMPS “D-TOUR / ORBIT / LOVELIGHT”); ROCHE BOBOIS (COFFEE TABLE “RADIAN”)
COURTESY OF THE DESIGNER (APPENDI-X-TABLE)

stockwerk3

This floor lamp with a tilt is called "drom tilt". It is energy efficient, can be pulled across the table, tilted towards the couch, or positioned pointing upright the ceiling. It received first place at the "goldener Stecker 2001" award of S.A.F.E. and the "red dot design award 2003."
"die 50 besten Schnitte" (the 50 best models) or how a Benjamin can be turned into something or something completely different. It includes 50 assembly instructions for how a single or several "Benjamin" stools by IKEA can be used to create new pieces of furniture - all Swiss descendants of the very popular "Benjamin."
"kokon" is an illumination object that changes according to the viewing angle. It was developed and implemented for the public realm.

» Conscious, sustainable and ingenious down to the smallest details. «

stockwerk3 designs, develops and produces lamps, illumination concepts, and room solutions tailored to individual needs and marketed through its own collection. Established in 1998, the company also offers single source sustainable concepts, design and production, or production support. The knowledge and expertise gained in the development and production of the collection is concientiously applied to all projects. In cooperation with the clients, mostly architecture or illumination planning companies or the public sector, they implement projects in the areas of illumination, interior design, and product development.

stockwerk3
«die 50 besten Schnitte»

PHOTOS: COURTESY OF THE DESIGNER

LABELFORM

The modern "Rocking Chair Steelnet SR830" is suited for indoor and outdoor use. A finely meshed steel net is stretched across its stainless steel frame. In combination with the matching seating cushion, there is nothing to stand in the way of many hours of reading enjoyment.

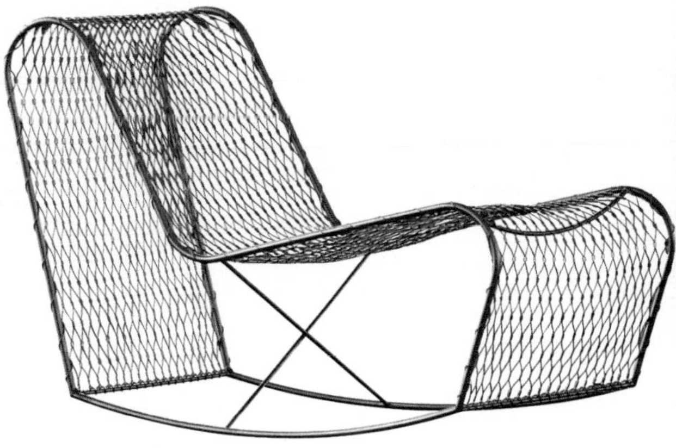

The shape of the sideboard ALU AS280 made of Alucobond has an attractive simplicity. Two drawers organize its inside. As it is available in several colors, it can be ordered to match any setting.

The simple shape of the "Sideboard Eternit ES 1900" matches every type of living room. Made of Eternit, it is supported by two stainless steel legs. It contains two drawers waiting to be filled.

Applying innovative materials to create functional furniture with a timeless style is the specialty of this young Swiss label. The process begins with a precise look at everyday furniture, whose shapes and functions are newly packaged by Labelform. The applied materials such as Alucobond, Eternit or stainless steel nets are unique in the furniture sector. Less is more - this is the guiding principle of Labelform when assigning shapes to their furniture. The simplicity of the products and the applied innovative materials aim to provide quality, long service life, and esthetics.

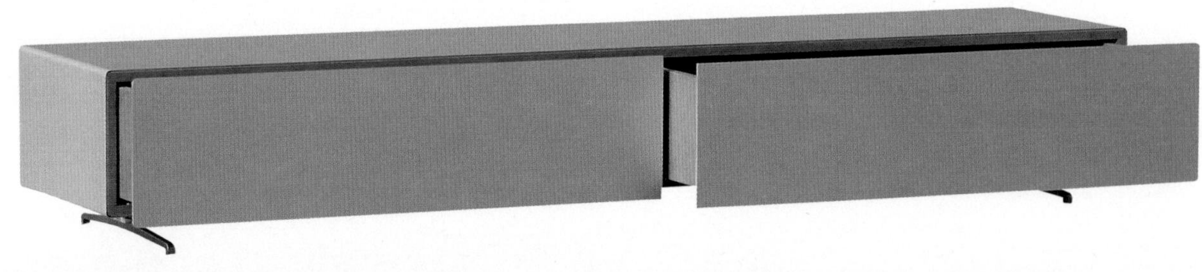

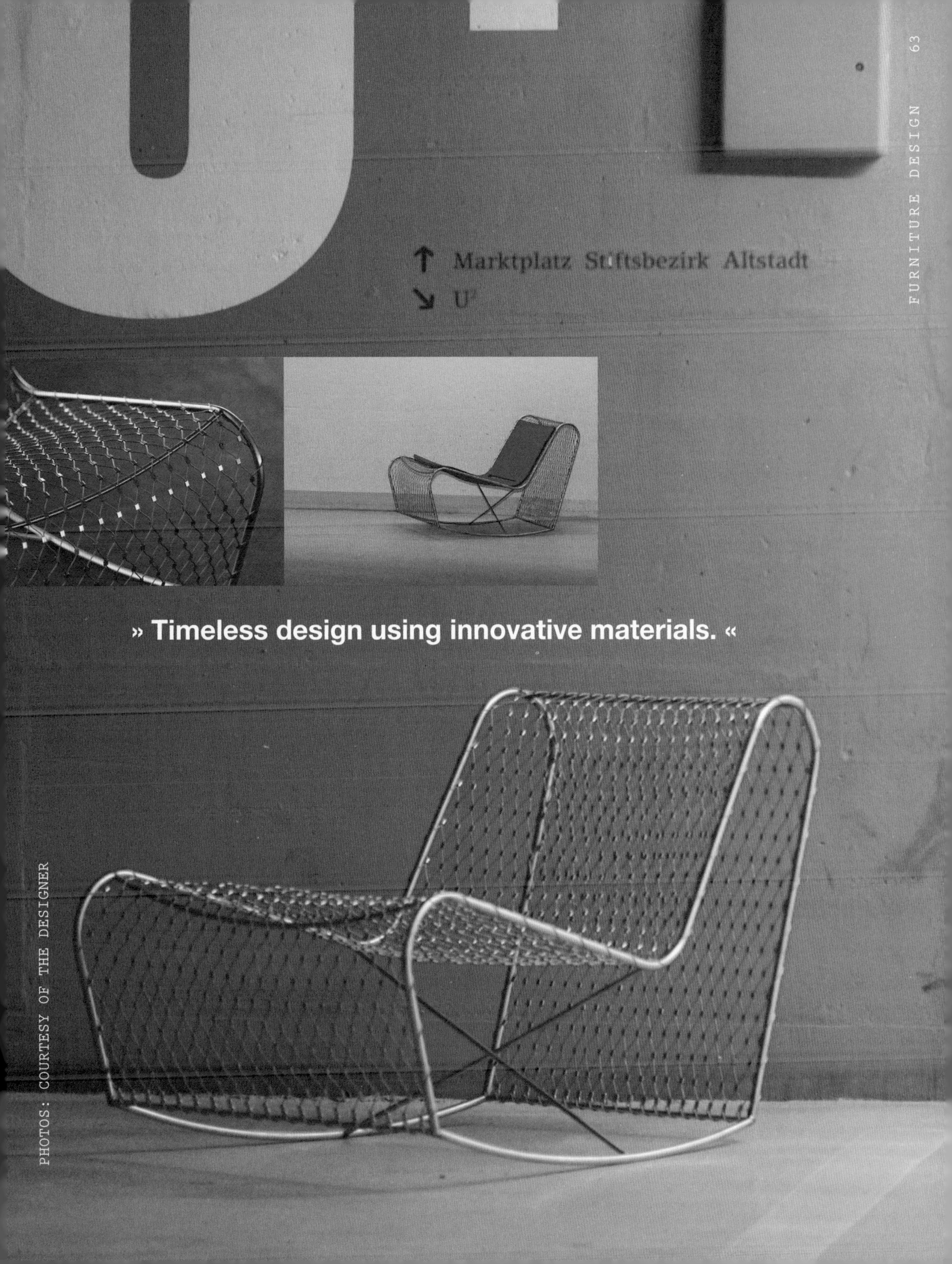

» Timeless design using innovative materials. «

PHOTOS: COURTESY OF THE DESIGNER

fries&zumbühl

"Steckling" consists of milled façade sheets that are fitted into each other to create a forked look reminiscent of the growth of plants.

The coat rack "captain hook" is a new interpretation of the classic bent wood coat rack from the art nouveau era. The flat, laser-cut individual parts and contrasting colors digress from the originals.

The "Waldhaus" series of lights is distinguished by simple shapes and natural materials. Authentic and simple, the lights provide warmth and sensuality to residential areas.

In the design process, one is confronted with content/form requirements as well as production and market-relevant needs. Ideas, esthetics, identity, originality, emotion, function, ergonomics, production, materials, innovation, ecology - whoever can confidently and securely maneuver within these parameters, their options and possibilities, can play with them. The studio fries&zumbühl assesses new values of these factors for every project. The rules and tools of the game are constantly redefined, while the designers act as players and referees.

» Clever, playful, durable with a poetic touch, yet always focused on the essential. «

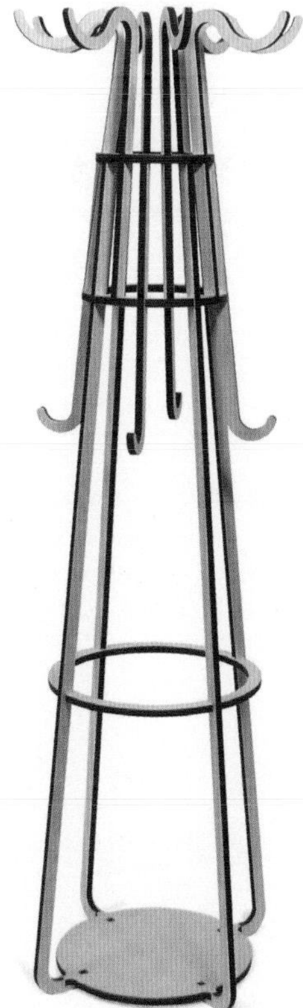

PHOTOS: COURTESY OF THE DESIGNER

KORB + KORB

"sense" is an office desk system that can be adjusted to the given spatial and functional conditions of any location. Intelligent modules render the design user-friendly and comprehensible. "sense" is perfectly suited to simple solutions for predefined configurations with a fresh esthetic appeal. The unique plug+play system allows the tool-free assembly of the furniture within seconds - it has never been easier to build a desk. "sense" is a modern piece of furniture that introduces esthetics and functionality to the work place.

» Success is never final. «
Winston Churchill

KORB + KORB is active in the areas of architecture, communication and design. In 1989 Susan D. and Daniel Korb established KORB + KORB in Stuttgart and in 1996 added a subsidiary in Baden/ Switzerland. In 1999 their scope of expertise was expanded to include communications. To KORB + KORB, design is more than the creation of a look for an object. The customer is successfully supported throughout the whole process from product development to marketing communications.

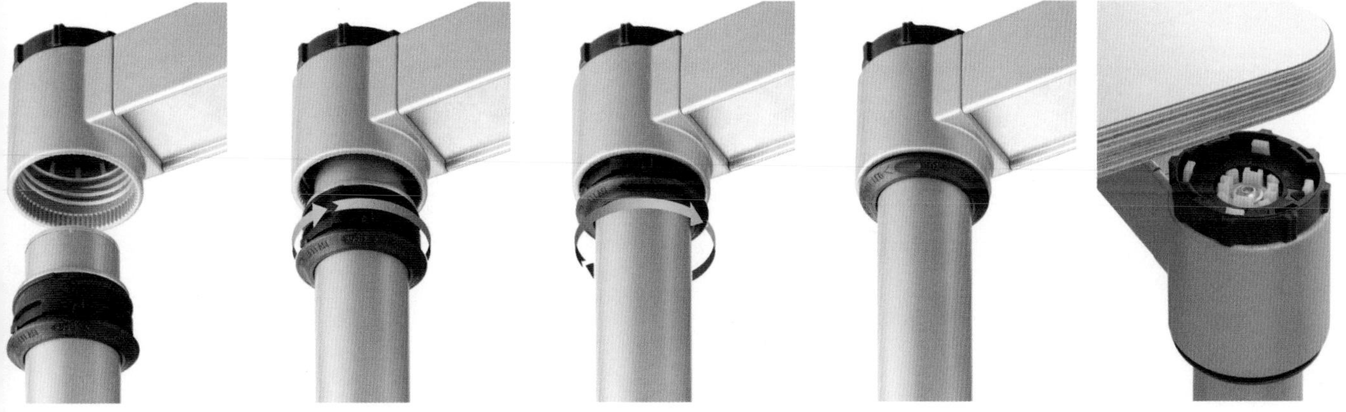

PHOTOS: COURTESY OF THE DESIGNER

PIURIC

The "SLIM Sofa" was conceived as a minimal sofa that is classic, light, elegant and sexy.
It is available from an easy chair with a length of 90 centimeters up to a couch of 220 centimeters in length. It offers the choice of a reclining extension attached either on the right or the left side. The frame consists of a plywood-steel construction with solid chrome steel skids.
"LOF" is a versatile module system that can be adjusted to any home setting. It includes a stool, easy chair, bench, recliner and chaise longue.

PIURIC, a young Swiss label, designs, plans and produces furniture.
The name PIURIC is synonymous with clear, timeless shapes. PIURIC also stands for design and implementation of spatial concepts and furniture with its own character.
To the label, development is synonymous with simplification, the quest for clear, simple shapes without affecting the function. As a Swiss manufacturer, the label produces very small series and customized solutions. Their motto is: not bigger and faster, but keeping it small and maintaining the level of quality.

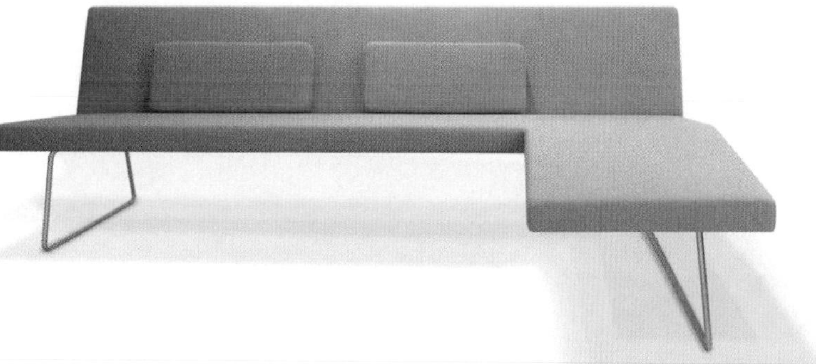

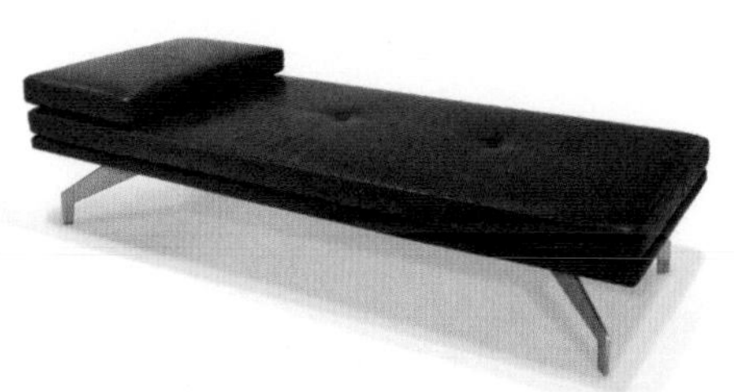

» Good design is conspicuously unobtrusive. «

PHOTOS: COURTESY OF THE DESIGNER

Florian Hauswirth

“JWC” is the acronym for Just Wood Chair which denotes a classic folding chair that consists exclusively of wood and has been produced without glue. “Loppa envelope” is a post-fossil lamp that has been inspired by letter envelopes.

The Sports Furniture collection is primarily intended for personal and physical fitness at home, while also serving as an unobtrusive, adjustable furniture collection. It is furniture with a dual use as a home accessory and fitness device.

Doubleface consists of a vase and a fruit bowl based on a mirrored silhouette. The bottom of the fruit bowl can be used as a chopping board.

» Good design combines shape and function, traditional craftsmanship, and new technologies, coupled with sustainability. «

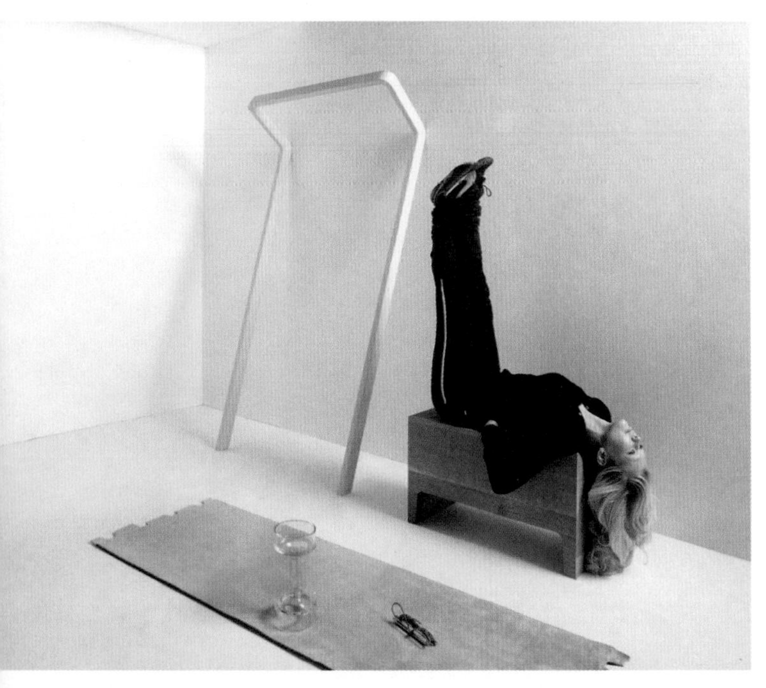

Florian Hauswirth studied industrial design at the FHNW, after completing his vocational training with a diploma in technical model construction. He gained initial work experience at Vogt+Weizenegger in Berlin and at BarberOsgerby in London. Between 2000 and 2007 he additionally worked as a model constructor and as a freelancer in material research for Vitra in Birsfelden before graduation. Florian Hauswirth is a founding member of POSTFOSSIL, a designer platform whose work wants to prepare us for the post-fossil era and sustainably design the future.

PHOTOS: FLORIAN HAUSWIRTH AND THOMAS WALDE, MIRIAM GRAF, NICI JOST

Pour les Alpes

The unique objects of the "echos" collection are a tribute to the Swiss Alps. In a formal and symbolical way, the furniture refers to an identity rooted in the traditional alpine culture. It tells exceptional new stories, which awake familiar memories but still offer room for interpretation. Referring to themes of reverence, curiosity and desire, which describe the designer's personal point of view of alpine characteristics, each piece of furniture has been elaborated with one carefully selected traditional technique such as carving, lace-making and shingle-making.

» Unique objects that trigger the imagination of the user «

Pour les Alpes is a cooperative of designers based in Zurich. Established in 2007 by the two designers Annina Gähwiler and Tina Stieger and inspired by traditional artisan methods and materials from specific regions, they create highly original and exclusive furniture and objects. Pour les Alpes seeks the individual and original properties of an object. Considering how the emotional and individual aspect of a piece of furniture that renders a handcrafted object into a unique collector's item can be expressed?

PHOTOS: TILL FORRER, ZÜRICH

Thomas Walde

"Trifoglio" is a simple enameled fruit bowl for indoor and outdoor use. The bowl is slightly curved to the inside, causing round fruit to always gather at its center. Its name is Italian for clover leaf.

"Charcoal pile table" - oiled oak wood pieces rotating along a circle are the basis of this simple living room glass table. No glue was needed due to the applied wood welding method. Its shape is reminiscent of charcoal burning and symbolizes a kiln in which the logs are conically stacked around a pole.

» A chair to ponder «

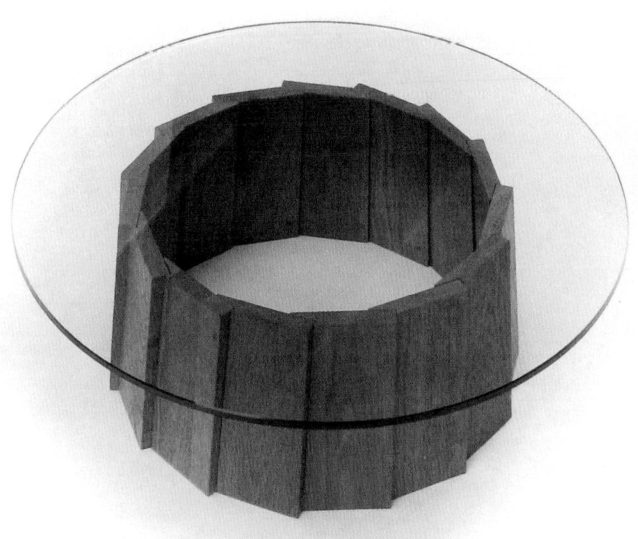

POSTFOSSIL is a platform of six designers who design and implement home decorations within the scope of diminishing resources and in anticipation of the post-fossil fuel era. However, POSTFOSSIL is more than just a label under which objects are created. POSTFOSSIL offers the young designers the opportunity to interact and exchange ideas. They search for responsibility within themselves and within each and every one of us. In their opinion, design is about more than just esthetics, it is about responsibility and the careful and long-sighted design of the future.

The chair, through its form, aims to encourage reflection and meditation which in this day and age is often suppressed by other activities. The reduction to structure and naked realisation activate the users and their thoughts. The size and high armrests, inspired by Le Corbusier's LC2, typically bring to mind an easy chair, however, it does not allow for much more than to sit down on it, meditate or open a book. The element in front of it corresponds to an ottoman which can also be used as repository or as a stool.

PHOTOS: REFLECT CHAIR AND OTTOMAN: PHILIPP HÄNGER

Graphic and Multimedia Design

Since the 1920s, Swiss graphic design has been distinguished by a clear and easily comprehensible style. Josef Müller-Brockmann, who taught together with Max Bill in Ulm, was among the best known representatives of this style. He created a new concept of page layout with grid systems. Swiss graphic design, however, will always remain linked to its key contribution to the history of typography. Based on the so-called new typography that attempted from the turn of the 20th century to overcome the unsystematic and ornamental variety of fonts, the Swiss typography school flourished after World War II. Frequently asymmetrical, rational sans serif fonts without ornamental elements in limited type sizes with large empty spaces are typical of this style. Adrian Frutiger, Emil Ruder, Max Miedinger and Karl Gerstner are among its most famous representatives. Frutiger, who worked in France for many years, developed an early version of the currently popular font named after him for Roissy airport in Paris. The Frutiger typeface as such was developed in 1975 as a sans-serif Linear Antiqua typeface. Frutiger's book „Der Mensch und seine Zeichen“ (1978) is to this day a standard work of applied semiotics in graphic design. However, the most famous Swiss typeface is a variation of Helvetica, developed in 1956 by the Zurich typographer Max Miedinger. It was newly arranged by Linotype under the name New Helvetica. To improve its depiction on computer monitors, Robin Nicholas and Patricia Saunders developed it into Arial for Monotype in 1990. This font has been incorporated in the Windows operating system since 1992. In Helvetica, the right leg of the upper case R initially extends straight downwards and then slightly curves while in Arial it extends diagonally, and the vertical bar of the lower case t ends horizontally in Helvetica and truncated in Arial. Even though the fonts only achieved international fame through the work of the two English typographers, both Helvetica and Arial remain essentially Swiss.

Büro Destruct

Available as iPhone application, desktop application and screensaver, BDD, Büro Destruct Designer creates an infinite number of randomly generated compositions from the graphic basic elements of circle, square and a number of rules. The user determines if the color combinations are created based on a harmonic concept or purely randomly. The desktop application and the iPhone application allow modification of the results and dispatching the compositions together with the color chart numbers via e-mail. The BDR A3MIK font includes the Latin alphabet, Japanese Katakana characters and Cyrillic letters.

The Bern-based graphic design team Büro Destruct (BD) was established in 1994. The services of BD for customers from very diverse segments are distinguished by a multitude of applied methods and humor. They include the design of corporate identities, logos and posters, font creation, illustration, product and character design, as well as animation & 3D. The Büro Destruct members are "MB" (Marc Brunner, 1970), "H1" (Heinz Reber, 1971), "HeiWid" (Heinz Widmer, 1967) and "Lopetz" (Lorenz Gianfreda, 1971).

» Small City – Big Design. «

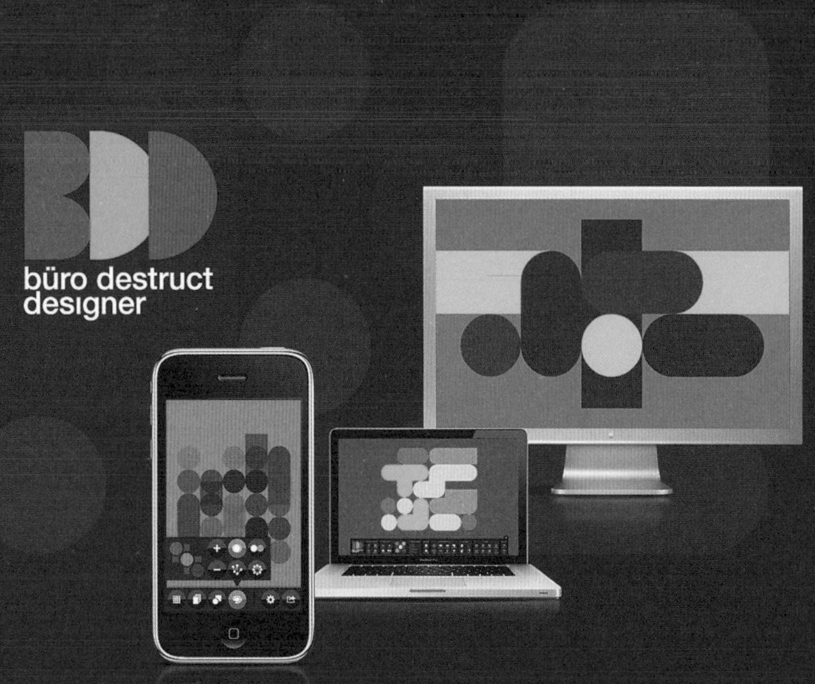

DOWNLOAD 3D HITBIT 24H
SONYA·LEIKA·PANAMONIC
OLYMPAS·CANYON·NOKIN
FUJIFILN·PENTIX·RIKOH
ACFA·COSIA·CODAK·SICMA
SUMSANG·SENY·TOSHIBU
EPSAN·KIOCERA·CANTOX
KANICO·MANOLTI·TOMRAN
RUDI·TAKINO·ZEISC·HUMA
KENGSTON·MUTZ·ROYNOX
ROLLUI·HENSO·DTK·KINKO
PALOROID·SAMDISK·PH

PHOTOS: COURTESY OF BÜRO DESTRUCT

HUBERTUS DESIGN

Hubertus Design operates an internal network club entitled "Hubertus Temporary", reviving the quarter legend. The club is an off-space, show, meeting and workshop space for the Hubertus-Design network as well as a semi-public culture, art and meeting venue.
After a four-month start-up phase, "Hubertus-Temporary" is already unparalleled. The unique variety of events coupled with the dogmatic stringency of its visual appearance resulted in a unique success story. The first product of the network is the club venue with its own tab. The series of event posters exhibit the skill of designers in handling typography and settings.

Hubertus Design is a design club of design and architecture specialists. With their extensive practical and sensory background they develop characteristic design and communications solutions and tailor them to the requirements of their customers. They approach conceptual projects with a heterogeneous configuration and apply a programmatic or pragmatic approach that is effectively implemented with the greatest attention to design and technical quality. Their work includes brand and editorial design, architecture, 3D-visualization, and web development.

» Art and design generate explications and implications of human thought, emotion, and action. « Moritz Moondgarten

Hubertus–Temporary Corporate Typeface

,.!?:;-–—/&%()[]*$

0123456789

abcdefgijklmnopqr

stuvwxyz

ABCDEFGIJKLMNO

PQRSTUVWXYZ

off–space

HOT

CLUB ZH

PHOTOS: CUSTOM-TYPEFACE «HUBERTUS» BY MARIETTA CONTESSA EUGSTER AND JONAS VOEGELI

CC | Carolina Cerbaro

The silkscreen poster "Weltraumvision" positions the writing and the picture in the present by its choice of colors. It contains a quote by the Russian Cosmonaut and space pioneer Juri Gagarin.

"Listen Nearby" is a mural painted on three wooden boards. The crystal structure of fluorite is repeated to create a totally new form. The rhythm is enclosed by a frame that allows the creation of a space.

» I know about constructive strength. Free implementation. «

Since graduating from university, Carolina Cerbaro has been working as an independent designer. Whether alone, or working on a group project, her work always has an artistic aspect, while the realms of art and culture are at the heart of her efforts. In 2009 she received the Eidgenössischer Förderpreis für Design (Swiss federal award for design).

The "Letraset carpet" features a series of fonts made of scratch letters. Fonts of diverse alphabet systems are exemplary woven into a carpet of letters and signs.

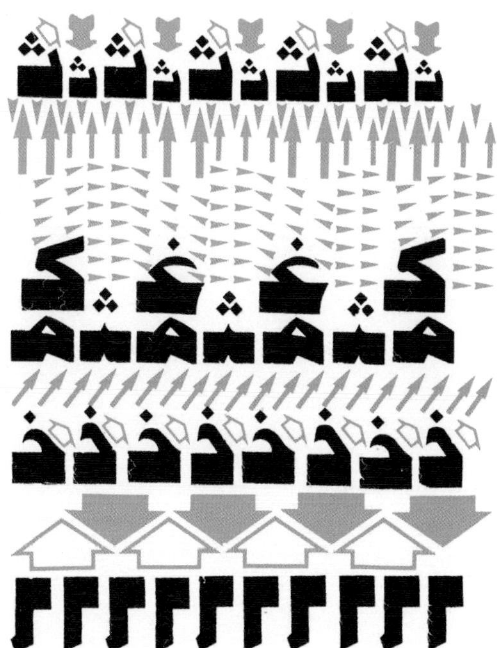

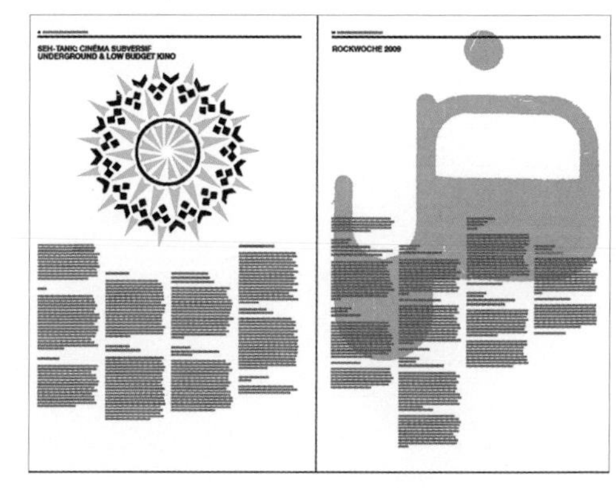

PHOTOS: COURTESY OF THE DESIGNER

Maximage Group

Maximage is involved in designing books, posters, flyers, T-shirts and different promotion materials for clients. Some of the projects use special digital tools for design and production. The magazine and poster named "Acid Test" for instance, is printed in 8 colors to explain offset printing possibilities to graphic design students. Other works employ really basic technologies, such as the limited edition poster made with marbled paper for the FTP group of artists.

Based in Lausanne and Zurich, Maximage Group is a company with a number of graphic designers, photographers, interior designers and artists working for different cultural and educational institutions. The goal of Maximage is to find non-conventional solutions to design and visual challenges.

» Lorem ipsum dolor sit amet lorem ipsum dolor sit « [sic]

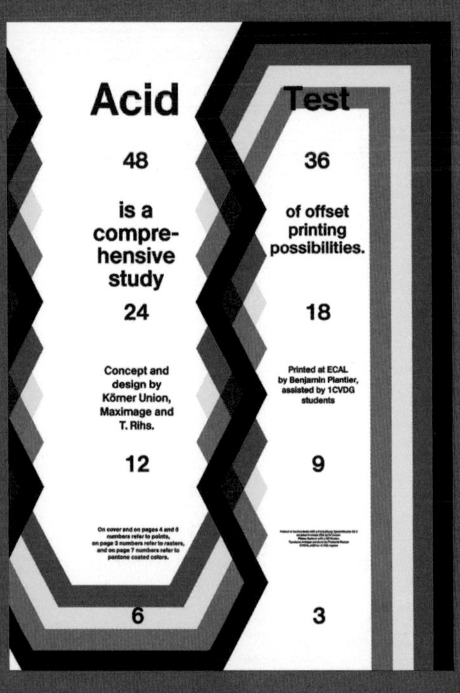

Swiss Design
—Typography
Learn Fast!
workshop 3/5/7 days
Private Lesson
Teacher in Swiss Univeristy of Design
Now in Brooklyn
Call (646) 409 8762
Swiss Design —Typography Call: 646 409 8762

PHOTOS: MAXIMAGE GROUP. ACID TEST WAS MADE IN C
OLLABORATION WITH FORMER UNION AND T. RHIS

Marie Lusa

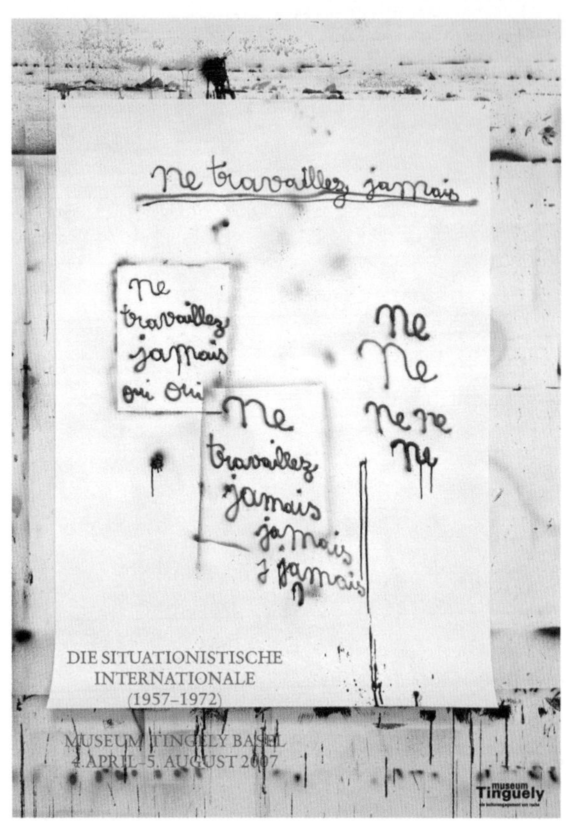

Marie Lusa has worked as a photographer, art director and graphic artist. For several years she established her own graphic design studio based in Zurich, which works for clients in the cultural and commercial sector with a focus on editorial design, communication systems, and brand identities. Recent projects include an exhibition book design “BASQUIAT” for Fondation Beyeler and the Musée d’Art Modern de la Ville de Paris; art direction and design for the new EPFL Diploma (Ecole polytechnique fédérale de Lausanne); editorial design for migros museum für gegenwartskunst Zurich and brand identity for the cabaret voltaire in Zurich. For Marie Lusa, each new project that she designs means delving into a new and unfamiliar world - and this challenge is her greatest driving force.

The designs by Marie Lusa alternate between creative art and applied graphics, abstract and concrete concepts, free sketching and strictly geometric styles. These poles - even the contradictions - can be present to various degrees in every project, while the subjective artistic expression dominates over the apparently objective design principles. The connection with the artist’s book, one of the sources of Marie Lusa’s inspiration, is clearly noticeable.

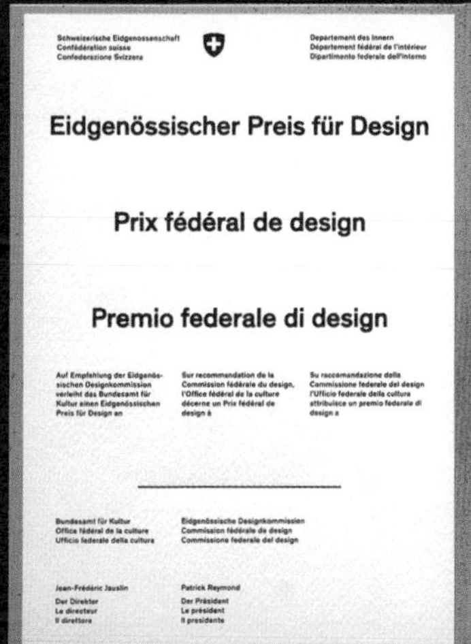

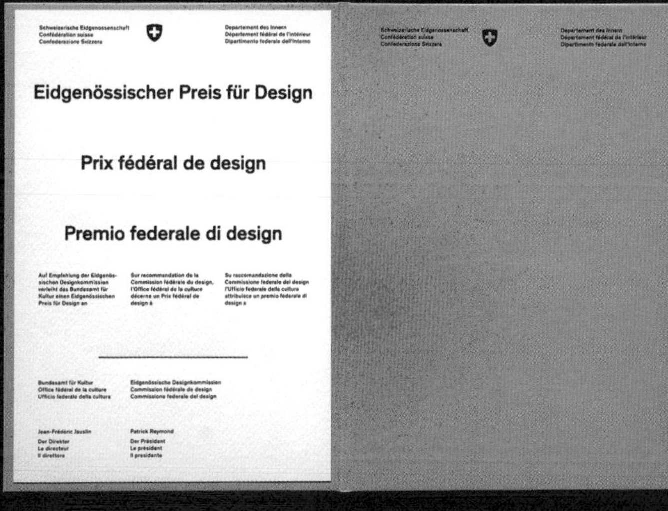

» Except for 3 or 4 bananas, there is no Dada, because Dada became Dada. «

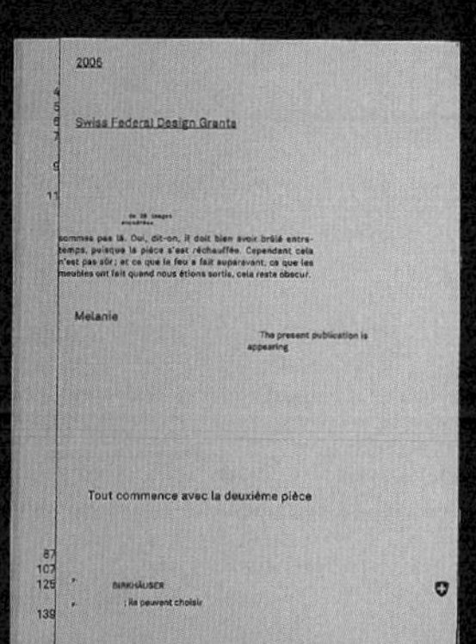

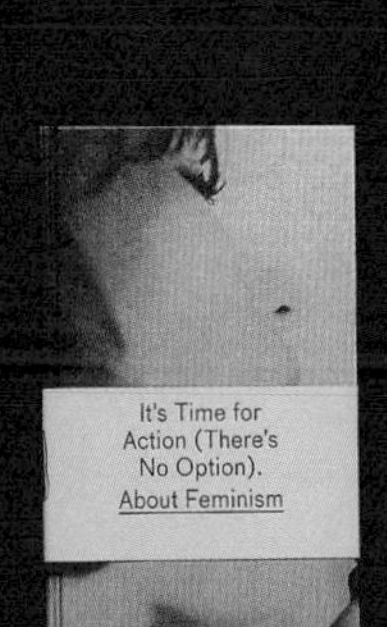

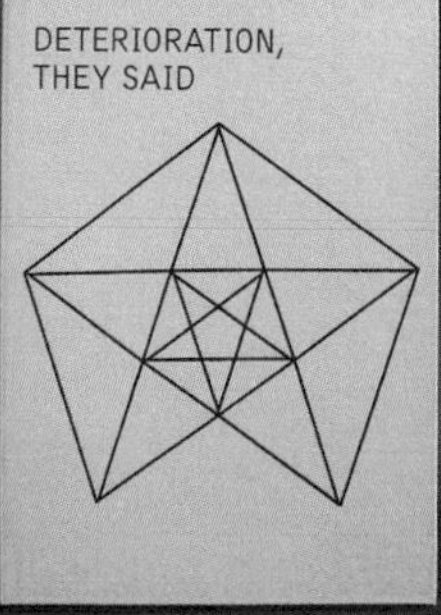

PHOTOS: MARIE LUSA

Elena Rendina

Elena Rendina envisions something and tries to give it a shape. She draws inspiration from everything that grabs her attention: furniture, textile patterns, paintings, etchings and so forth. Every object, reference, decontextualized and decomposed becomes abstract and a raw material ready to be worked on. Creating images becomes a ground for experimentation, creation, originality. And the models become actors, characters of a world out of time, a world that doesn't exist and that never existed although it refers to real things. The photographer attempts to create and build all elements of the frame: clothing, setting, objects.

» Less is less, more is more. «

Elena Rendina is a photographer, set designer and costume designer. She visited the Liceo Artistico until 2004 and studied Visual Communication/ Photography afterwards at the ECAL, University of Art and Design in Lausanne. Between 2006 and 2010 she held several exhibitions, received various awards and worked with Paolo Roversi and Shona Heath. She attempts to build all the elements enclosed in the frame: clothing, setting, objects.

PHOTOS: ELENARENDINA@ECAL

Regula Stüdli

Jungle Friends - pattern monsters, magic flowers and striped patterns thrive in the jungle of a 3D graffiti. Nominated in 2009 for the Swiss Design Award, the work was conceived by Regula Stüdli as an installation upon invitation from Tuchinform of Winterthur. The unique style of the fabric designer is present throughout the crazy-colored-candy cosmos. Analog and digital design motifs, symbols and patterns with a vibrant vitality - hand sketched, photographed and sampled, are printed via inkjet on fine polyester quality material and covered with a light-reflecting hologram foil. The combination of innovative technology and design become a colorful feast for the senses. Welcome to the jungle!

Regula Stüdli creates her independent work projects at her studio in St. Gallen. The research of innovative design solutions is the theme that extends throughout her professional life. In her diploma thesis entitled "Ink Jet Printing", she presented scenarios dealing with the holistic approach to design and technical implementation as mutually dependent processes. After being nominated for the Swiss Design Award 2001 she worked as a fabric designer at Jakob Schlaepfer, where she pursued this approach in an innovative setting.

» And this was the beginning of a beautiful friendship. «

PHOTOS: CANDY CIRCLE, INSTALLATION JUNGLE FRIENDS, REGULA STÜDLI, ST. GALLEN
AUSSTELLUNG DESIGN PREIS SCHWEIZ 2009, INSTALLATION JUNGLE FRIENDS, FOTOGRAF DANIEL SUTTER, ZÜRICH
THE JUNGLE FRIENDS, INSTALLATION JUNGLE FRIENDS, REGULA STÜDLI, ST. GALLEN

Dessert

Since the opening of Club Zukunft 2006 in Zurich, Atelier Dessert has redesigned the wall decorations of the entire premises every year. Applying specially designed stencils, developed in-house, parts of the wallpaper are illuminated with glossy foil that reflects the light when the club is in operation.

Made of industrial felt, the product "cc-lush" (calculated chaos-lush) emerged from the concept of being able to plant individual areas. The modular connector system consists of six different individual parts and is magnetic.

The design studio Dessert was established in 2004 by fabric designer Patricia Wicky and graphic designer Fabian Stacoff in Zurich. The name stands for fine creations that are developed with great attention to detail in the small workshop.
In addition to graphic design, fabric designs and patterns, the studio also develops wall and entire room decorations and implements them with various techniques. The credo of the studio is: Dessert makes you happy, don't you also want a piece of the cake?

» Dessert is synonymous with delicate design creations that are developed with great attention to detail. «

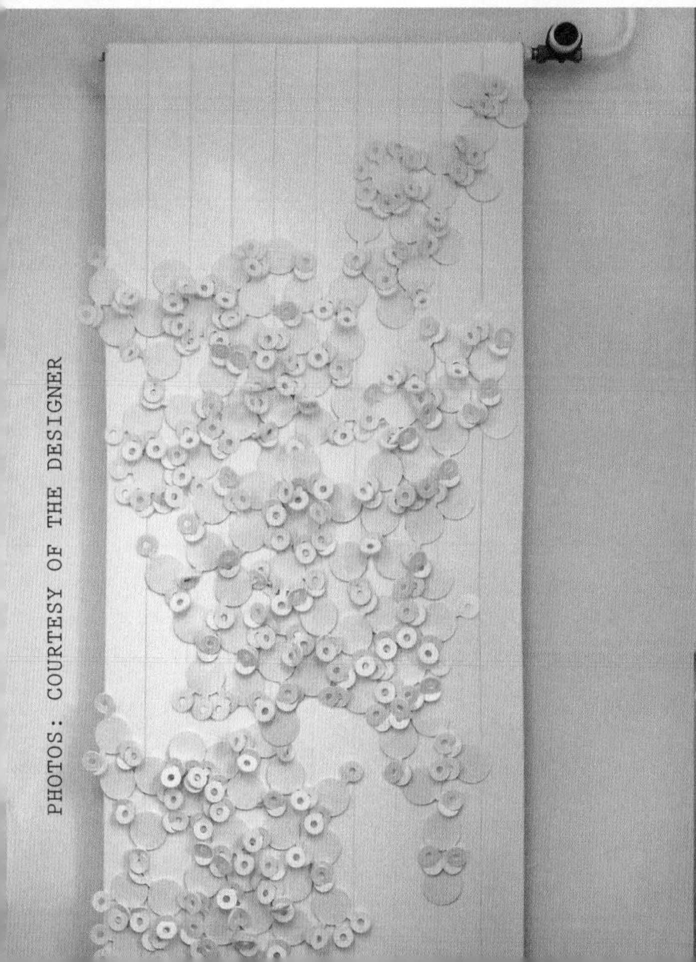

PHOTOS: COURTESY OF THE DESIGNER

Remo Caminada

Always in search of adequate and new exciting forms of expression, Remo Caminada allows individual assignments to inspire his work. When designing posters he applies typography in an illustrative way that blends design and information into a single visual unit. The use of bright colors at the center contrasts with the usually dark background, providing the posters with a plastic effect and dynamism. The business card, commissioned by a dental office illustrates how the constant search for new conceptual and production methods leads to remarkable outcomes.

The office of graphic designer Remo Caminada is unconventional in the way that it adjusts to his life and moves wherever he goes. He considers the constant search for and discovery of the unknown to be an important core essence for creative work, allowing him to develop new and unconventional ideas. The credo of his client-related work is: the best cooperation results when the client sees me as a creator and not only a service provider - and if in return I consider the client to be a partner with an interesting concern.

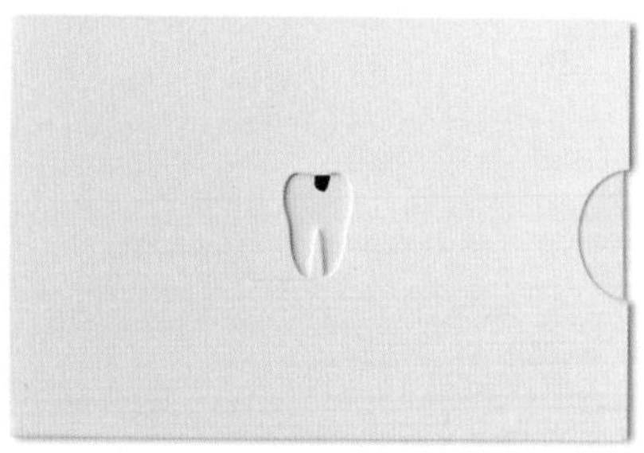

» Swiss graphic design in the 1950s, 1960s and 1970s used to be 0°/45°/90°, now it is perhaps 22.34°/39.99°/-68.03°. «

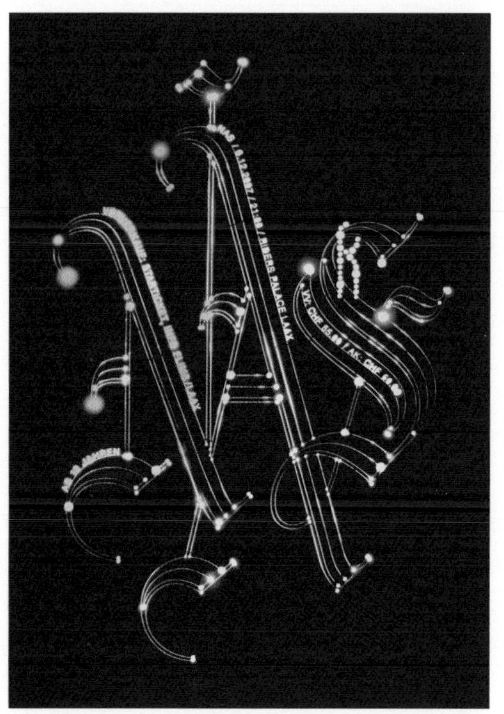

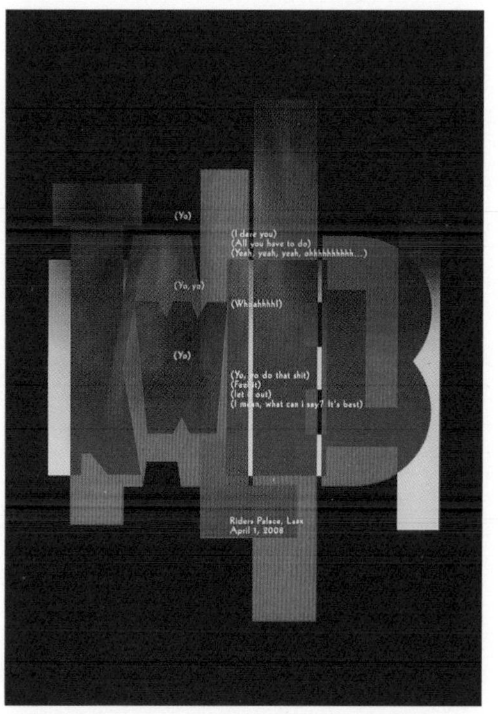

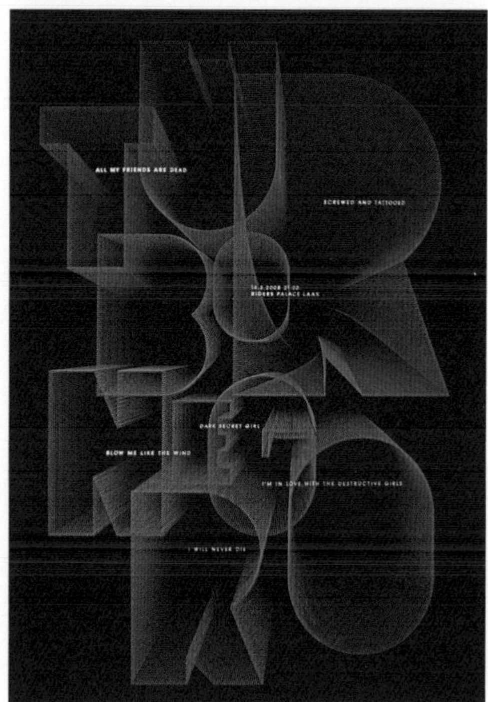

PHOTOS: REMO CAMINADA

Schaffner & Conzelmann designersfactory

With plan b, Coop Schweiz tries to lure the generation of under twenty-year-olds into shopping center. The powerful graphic design contains graffiti and tattoo elements and offers a flexible module kit for various packages. With "Fine Food Design", Coop Schweiz offers high-quality kitchen aids whose packaging with esthetic images and black/silver sections reflects the key elements of the fine food line while conveying the feel of a special lifestyle.

Schaffner & Conzelmann was established in 1976 as an individual company and in 1987 turned into a corporation, based in Basel. Designersfactory consists of a core team of designers with many years of experience in all sectors of visual communication and brand design. The company incorporates a photo studio, illustrators, photo editors and its own pre-press department. Established 34 years ago, the company has gathered experience in all areas of business, industry, service and trade. It currently provides services to 60 customers and implements 600 projects annually.

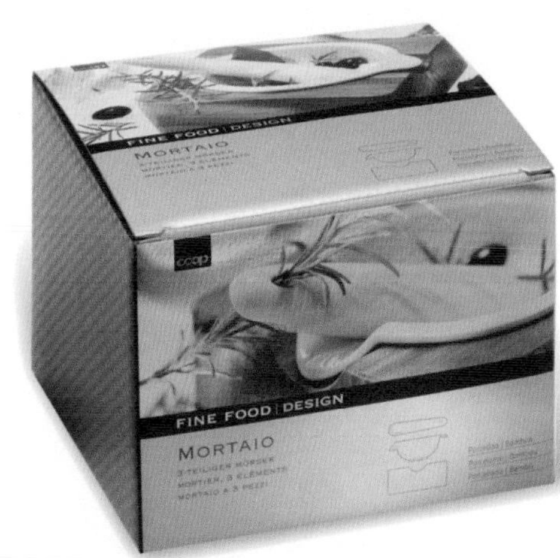

» The feel of a special lifestyle «

PHOTOS: SCHAFFNER & CONZELMANN, DESIGNERSFACTORY.COM

Fauxpas Grafik

The appearance of the nature museum in Winterthur is based on a modular system. Predefined design elements can be used to continuously develop the building's visual appearance, while maintaining its identity and recognition value.

Fauxpas Grafik independently designs corporate and institutional presences. The company attempts to individually comply with the needs of its clients to communicate their contents in a clear and visually appealing language. The wide range of expertise includes the areas of corporate design, editorial design, conception and implementation of websites, exhibition design, signage and packaging design.

» Modular design — is what we like. «

PHOTOS: COURTESY OF THE DESIGNER

9·6

9·6, Conceptual Worlds, specializes in the corporate communications sector. The creative company develops a multifaceted range of communication tools focusing on the nature and needs of the client and often informed by issues from the world of art. On the one hand, reflections and discourses within visual arts prize open blocked thoughts; on the otherhand, sensitivity is mobilized exactly where individuality becomes perceptible in collective society. For their work as information designers in the development of high-quality print and multimedia, these are no doubt important, concomitant factors that shape and underpin the company's unique approach.

9·6 is the brainchild of a team of passionate communicators with different preferences and talents - designers, copywriters and conceptual designers - who have been joyfully strutting along the fields of corporate communications for years. Their work does not reflect an agency-own style, but allows the indigenous parameters, people and worlds of a project to provide perpetually new inspirations and accents. Thus, the correct vessel is created for every message. The approach of 9·6 is not reflected in a uniform style but in the quality of the delivered work. 9·6 is in touch with the arts scene.

» The source of individual charisma for a collective perception lies within ourselves. «

PHOTOS: NIKLAUS BÜRGIN, DONATA ETTLIN, PHILIPPE HOLLENSTEIN, MATTHIAS WILLI

Jewelry Design

Watches and jewelry are Switzerland's third most important industry and Baselworld is the sector's largest and most important trade fair on a global scale. Independent goldsmiths constitute the backbone of Swiss jewelry production. Their very diverse pieces reflect the different natures of the three main linguistic regions - as strict as Germany, as opulent as Italy, and as traditional as France, but always of very high quality. Goldsmiths complete four years of professional training optionally followed by a design degree from a university of applied sciences. A sector dominated by brands and series, Swiss watches are probably the epitome of Swiss precision craftsmanship. Watchmakers also complete three years of professional training. In the past, watches were produced in rural areas during winter time, which is why many renowned manufacturers are still located in rural regions. In 1601, the "Meisterschaft der Uhrmacher von Genf" (Association of Geneva watchmakers) was established. However, wristwatches, the backbone of the Swiss watch industry, were not invented until the late 18th century in England. In 1927 Rolex introduced an absolutely waterproof wristwatch. The general luxury product crisis of the 1970s and the competition from Far

East severely affected the Swiss watch industry. Nevertheless, the Swiss share of global production in terms of value is once again at 50 percent, which includes not only luxury watches but also the most popular “cheap watch.” Containing only a few parts, as compared to over 300 parts in luxury watches, Swatch watches with their diverse looks and designer editions were able to establish a totally new market - affordable watches and quickly changing collections, small designer editions and special series that are produced in sync with the market. They combine mass production with the nearly individual production style of the goldsmiths discussed above.

formabina schmuckgestaltung

The apparently random intertwining of the "Sphaira" collection is actually systematic. Each of the six identical blossoms determines the location of the others through its quintuple radial symmetry. They mutually affect each other, to shape the light body of the blossom sphere. While the ring shank of "Velvel" takes a three-quarter turn, there is simultaneously a smooth transition between circle and square. The Spirit Diamond and the Context Diamond create shiny accents at the ends. In the "Circulus" ring, several curved circular discs with graded diameters are loosely placed on top of each other inside the lentoid body. Movement causes the discs to rotate while a diamond orbits at the center.

» Modern jewelry culture between concrete construction, playful lightness and emotional sensuality. «

The Swiss designer Bettina Geistlich develops and creates innovative jewelry under the brand name formabina schmuckgestaltung. In her work the interplay of shape, material and method is conceived as an inseparable unit. One cannot be imagined without the other. Her simple and coherent, clear and consistent designs are worn by modern people with the highest demands for sophisticated designs, high-quality materials and perfect finishing. The formabina collection is available at select national and international jewelers.

PHOTOS: CIRCULUS UND SPHAIRA: ROLAND SPRING
VELVEL: SANDRA STAMPFLI

Esther Brinkmann BIJOUX

"The last drop" is a glove with a pearl shaped like a drop attached to the tip of the middle finger. It symbolizes the moment before separation, a fleeting point in time, which can become endless.

The "red face" series is based on the designer's perception of China. They feature the different faces which make up a personality. They discuss identity, the individual within the mass, the original among the copy.

The designer is very much involved in creating things that have a specific relationship to the body. They underline our attitudes and needs in life - meaningful activities and relationships, relaxing and spiritual moments, emotion and beauty. Since her graduation in 1978, Esther Brinkmann has worked for numerous private and public collections. She has extensive international teaching and lecturing experience and currently works and lives in Guangzhou, China.

» Not just for your body «

Pretty much as a vase contains and values a flower, a ring contains and values a finger. "Fingervessels" not only create a space between the ring and the finger but also the spaces between fingers.

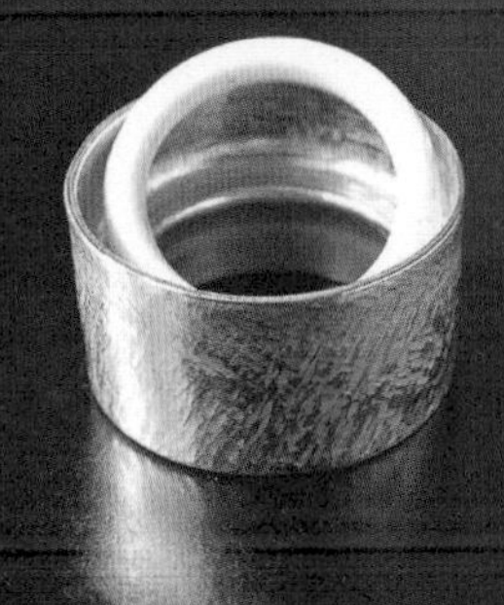

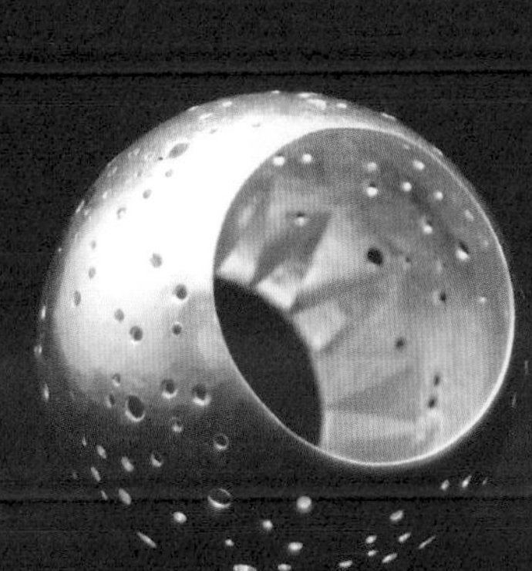

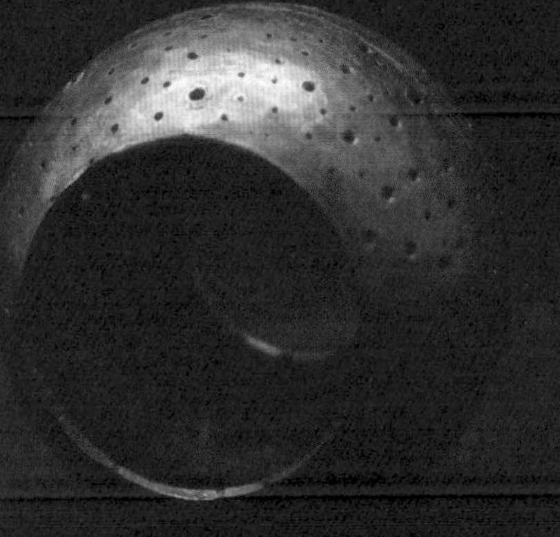

PHOTOS: XUPEIWU, GOGOGO, ESTHER BRINKMANN

Rado

With its curved silhouette, "Rado True Sport" is the new sports model of this contemporary high-tech ceramics collection. "Sintra Skeleton Automatic", a limited edition of 222 watches, has a particularly esthetic appeal with the black visible automatic movement in the black streamlined case. Conceived in collaboration with the British designer Jasper Morrison, the white ceramics watch band of "r5.5 White Jubilé" perfectly merges with the case. "eSenza Blue Jubilé" is captivating with its elegant elliptic shape and sapphires arranged in accordance to the Fibonacci numbers. In the successor of the classic model of 1989, the "Ceramica Digital Automatic", the clock face, slightly curved sapphire glass, case, and watch band are all seamlessly blended.

Rado belongs to Swatch Group's premium brands and known for timeless design and high-tech materials based on extensive material research activities. The use of sapphire crystal, high-tech ceramics, and even high-tech diamonds strongly and uniquely distinguishes Rado watches, securing numerous international design awards for the brand. Established in 1957, the history of Rado shows a remarkable number of pioneering innovations. One of the certainly most spectacular is the creation of the "high-tech diamond", resulting from the conversion of carbon into a nanocrystalline diamond, the world's hardest material for the world's hardest watch.

» Iconic design — pure design — modern design. «

PHOTOS: RADO

Natalie Luder

» The prepared dish always also refers to its immanent end and is, in fact, an artificial state between life and decay. « (Ursula Peters)

The art project "Das Jagdessen" (hunter's dinner) features jewelry created from the teeth of 125 rabbits. The pieces created from approximately 3,500 teeth resemble trophies. They have an alluring beauty that only causes slight discomfort upon a closer inspection. The staging of these objects as part of a baroque feast at which the actual 125 rabbits were served, intended to include various art forms and combine them into a single unique work of art. Overall, four necklaces, a pendant, approximately ten brooches, and several stud earrings were created, each one of them one-of-a-kind.

Through her work the designer and artist examines the status of jewelry and related materials in society. In this sense she prefers doing jewelry research than market-oriented jewelry design. Her work is often inspired by topics of food culture. The juxtaposition of appearance and reality or nature and culture result in aspects that never cease to fascinate her and can be applied to both food and ornaments.

PHOTOS: CPHOTOS SCHMUCK: NATALIE LUDER
FILMSTILLS FROM "DAS JAGDESSEN" BY NORA DE BAAN

Simone Gugger

Jewelry made by **Simone Gugger** often only reveals its secret at a second glance. A closer look reveals stories in the poetic, unique one-of-a-kind objects. Her jewelry pieces have a clear beauty and are traditionally handcrafted. The choker 'Duvetgebirge' (Duvet mountain range') from the 'Lichtblicke' series encircles the neck of the wearer with the panorama picture of a mountain range. Framed in a silver frame between

» The familiar removed from the frame of the conventional, in sensuous vicinity to the body. «

two glass sheets, the apparent snowy peaks are actually folds of the cover and stuffing of a comfortably warm duvet. The collection also includes earrings and cufflinks whose illustrations are implemented with various methods.

At a venue where gear wheels were once manufactured, Simone Gugger has been creating jewelry for the past ten years. The studio of the jewelry designer is located in the industrial ambiance of the Maag premises in the direct vicinity of a number of other creative small businesses. The light-flooded high rooms are her testing grounds, production site and store all in one. She designs and creates rings, cufflinks, and ear and neck jewelry models in small series. This allows her to respond to customer wishes, which is particularly popular for wedding bands.

PHOTOS: SIMONE GUGGER

Swatch

In the mid 1970s, the Swiss watch making sector experienced an acute crisis caused by its Asian competitors. Only the revolutionary idea of the "Second Watch" by Nicolas G. Hayek led the sector out of its massive decline and established today's classic status of Swatch watches. The basic premise was to create plastic watches that did not cost a fortune as opposed to pieces of expensive jewelry craftsmanship. The brightly colored watches were intended to match the different personalities of their wearers, reflect their emotions, and suit various fashions. New materials are used for the range of Swatch products - from plastic via stainless steel to synthetic fibers, rubber and silicone.

» Innovation, provocation, enthusiasm. Forever. « Nicolas G. Hayek

Since Nicolas G. Hayek surprisingly introduced in 1983 the first original Swatch called "Once Again," leading the Swiss watch making industry out of its digital watch crisis, more than 350 million Swiss-made "Second Watches" have been produced. New methods are constantly being developed for the manufacturing of Swatches, while renowned designers repeatedly conceive new models. This is made possible by the radical reduction of the number of pieces of a watch - the "Revolution 51." Advanced micro-electronics and sophisticated software technology additionally contribute new functions such as RFID chips to the watches, allowing them to be used as electronic tickets for accessing mountain railways, stadiums, or public transportation.

PHOTOS: COURTESY OF SWATCH LTD.

daughter of eve, eva katharina bruggmann

The "Love rings" are mobile finger rings that are suitable for play. They consist of five different ring models with ball-bearing constructions in which the arrangement of the balls corresponds to Braille writing. The "letter rings" are signet rings reflecting the world of our language. This series includes three different styles - touch type, privy seal, and courier 10. The "precious stone-ball-rings" are eight different models that offer perfect accessories for every occasion, matching any type of outfit. The gemstone ball can be exchanged at will. The size of the gemstone ball determines the ring size.

At her studio in Zurich, Eva Katharina Bruggmann - trained goldsmith, gemologist and designer - creates extraordinary pieces of jewelry of the highest quality under the label daughter of eve. She produces small series for select individuals with exclusive taste and a sense for lasting values. Her focus is on timeless jewelry that will never lose its charm. The small series are handcrafted and carefully finished. Thus every ring is produced with the highest attention like a unique piece and turned into a noble piece of jewelry.

PHOTOS: SAMUEL KÜNZLI, ZÜRICH (SCHWEIZ)

» Design is the attempt to make the intangible tangible. «

Luzia Vogt

Once old coins lose their monetary value they are turned into pieces of jewelry. The value and the embossed symbol are no longer legible after the process, only the coin. The embossing is reduced to an individual section, a human aspect.
Similarly, discarded combs are turned into pieces of jewelry. Their origin is only visible upon a second glance. Serial industrial products are given an organic touch by the intervention.
For “I am hungry” the basic shape of a simple bowl is slightly altered and a plaster mould created which is then cast in porcelain. The plaster mould is changed via a spoon after each casting series.

In her work, Luzia Vogt focuses on the unintentional passing on of items - i.e. on finding and reacting to what is found. She discovers used objects, usually serial products, picks them up, collects and organizes them. She then uses the objects as basic material, approaching the properties of this material through various experiments. The approach matches the properties of each object. She interferes, alters, and leaves traces. Every process is irreversible.

» Haste makes waste. «

PHOTOS: LUZIA VOGT, BASEL; PETRA JASCHKE, PFORZHEIM

Omega

Created in 1957, the "Speedmaster" with manual wind movement is distinguished by its arrow-shaped hands, matte black face, and satined stainless steel bezel with an engraved tachymeter scale. In the early 1960s, NASA decided to equip its astronauts with wrist chronographs. Only the "Speedmaster" by OMEGA was able to weather the extreme conditions, becoming the official NASA watch in 1965. Thereafter it accompanied astronauts into space and was part of the first moon landing in 1969. In the following year the watch participated in the rescue of Apollo 13, for which it received the "Snoopy Award" by NASA. At that time it received its nickname, the "Moon Watch."

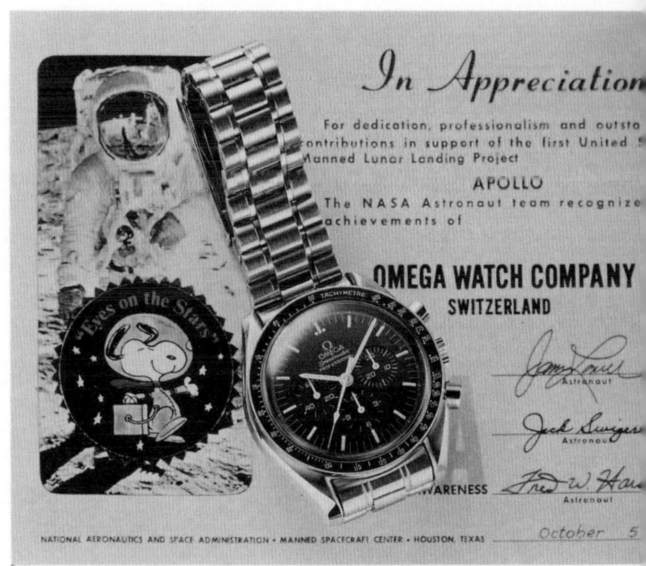

» The First Watch worn on the Moon «

In 1848, Louis Brandt opened a watchmaker workshop in La Chaux-de-Fonds, Switzerland. In 1879, his sons transformed the company into a workshop in Biel and in 1894 the name OMEGA was used for the first time for a pocket watch. In 1932, OMEGA watches were used for the first time for official timing of the Olympic Games. The brand continuously introduced new innovations - Omega watches survived six moon landings, were the first diving watches and the world's only wrist watches with marine chronometer certification. On the occasion of the 35th anniversary of the last Apollo space expedition, in 2010 OMEGA is introducing its Speedmaster Professional Apollo-Soyuz "35th Anniversary," with a clock face made of meteorite material.

PHOTOS: OMEGA

Product Design

Swiss products are generally associated with quality and quality products are distinguished by their appearance. Therefore, initially, the look of products turns buyers into buyers of Swiss products. The design must convey the quality of the product, its material and its function. Yet product design is much more than an outward shape. Product design also determines the shape of the function and must therefore go hand in hand with product development. Just as the line between development and design is diminishing, it is also being eliminated between industrial and handcrafted styles. Even designers without formal professional training increasingly aim at highest design perfection. The fact that this has always been the case in Switzerland becomes apparent in classic items with presumably anonymous designs, such as the Swiss army knife, the vegetable economy peeler Rex or the Davos sled. Swiss product designers obviously favor clear shapes that are not necessarily stylish but always classy. However, this does not mean that right-angled cubes dominate their styles, but rather interrupted, wedged or pointed shapes are frequently found. Of course there are also bimorph product designs with the associated variety of uses - such as Willy Guhl's concrete garden chair of 1954. In both variations, Swiss design does not aim for the Olympic “higher, faster, further,” but instead they aim at “more humane, functional, and elegant.” Sustainable design is another area of emphasis - products with longer service lives, ecological raw materials and resource-friendly production methods constitutes buying incentives as much as “Die gute Form” (“The good shape”). This was the title of a traveling exhibition conceived by Max Bill in 1949, which provided public information in the era of the budding design profession. Today, a good design has become an essentially quality of every good product.

Victorinox

The Swiss “Army Officers’ Knife” by Victorinox is the classic among pocket tools. It is the light, and primarily more elegant, version of the soldiers’ knife with additional functions. Company founder Karl Elsener used the cross and shield, today’s emblem, to differentiate his products from those of his competitors. Today, the “Officers’ knife” is available in more than 100 variations and combinations. The series is topped by the top model “SwissChamp”

» Fresh, innovative and different. Swiss design constitutes today’s modernity. «

with 33 functions, consisting of 64 individual parts, the knife weighs only 185 grams. It has been successfully tested even in extreme situations such as mountain tops and tropical forests.

Together with other cutlers, Karl Elsener began in 1890 to manufacture soldiers' knives for the army. His approximately 25 colleagues gave up after an industrial manufacturer in Germany began to offer the knives more cost effectively. Only Karl Elsener persisted, losing his entire fortune in the process. In 1909, following the death of his mother, Karl Elsener chose her first name Victoria as the brand name for his factory. When stainless steel, which was invented in 1921, was also introduced in his native town of Ibach, Inox, the international code for stainless steel was added to the name of the stainless steel knives of the "Victoria" brand. The combination of the two words resulted in today's brand and company name Victorinox.

PHOTOS: COURTESY OF THE DESIGNER

Heiko Hillig

Cats for bambinis - when the teeth are on their way, babies can safely explore the natural oak wood with their mouth. Attached to the baby carriage, little hands rotate the kitty, while the pacifier remains within reach thanks to the clip.
The brushed aluminum has a silken glow. Like a thin frame, it encloses the walnut wood in the lid of bottom of these purist boxes - a noble casing for little treasures. Stacked layers of paper wrapped in color - the designer developed a very unique technique for his “abstract compositions.” As an exhibition visitor once said: “Material, color, viewing angle, a phenomenon of perception - and the light with all its warmth to boost, can anyone fail to hear the music?”

Heiko Hillig is active in many areas of design. His portfolio ranges from product design via graphic design and catalog conception to product photography and text. Toy design is certainly one of his areas of specialization. In cooperation with the well-known Naef company, he has already implemented many of his designs. The principle of “simple shapes for a wealth of ideas” is consistently present in his toy designs. He also reached fame as an independent artist - he created the “Schweizer Bund” (Swiss Federation), a wooden sculpture with great symbolic meaning situated at the highway border crossing of Rheinfelden.

» Design is attitude. «

PHOTOS: COURTESY OF THE DESIGNER

fuseproject

For Nicholas Negroponte's One Laptop Per Child (OLPC) organization, fuseproject designed the world's first $100 "XO" laptop aimed at bringing education and technology to the world's poorest children. "HBF C. Collection curve" is a collection of lounge, reception and private sitting area furnishings in a clean contemporary style. The Bluetooth headset "Jawbone PRIME" in Earcandy colors combines audio quality, comfort, and fresh colors, turning the audio equipment into a piece of jewelry. "Anima Terra" is a sculptural landscape illuminated by LEDs from the inside.

fuseproject was established in 1999 by the Swiss industrial designer Yves Béhar as a design and branding company in San Francisco. The studio is focused on humanistic design and the "giving" element of the profession, with the goal of creating projects that are deeply in-tune with the needs of a sustainable future, connected with human emotions, and that enable self-expression. Yves Béhar's work has been the subject of two solo exhibitions as well as being included in the permanent collections of international museums worldwide, such as the MOMA, the Musee d'Art Moderne/Pompidou Center, the Chicago Art Institute and the Munich Museum of Applied Arts.

» Design brings stories to life. «

PHOTOS: FUSEPROJECT

Revox

The tradition of top-quality audio equipment continues today with a modular, upgradable technology concept. The "Re:system M100" is a system for life, which can grow over time to meet changing expectations. New modules, even including future technology, are simply plugged into a bus and the new functions are recognized and registered automatically. With is characteristic black glass front and a surface of brushed stainless steel, the "M100" has an elegant and high-quality look. Metal or leather in many colors, wood and even sheet gold are available as alternative surfaces. Control is possible through an iPhone, WLan or MS Windows. The "M100" can supply a maximum of 32 rooms with different music in 4 listening zones.

The audio system´s manufacturer was established in 1948 by Swiss native Willi Studer, initially to produce tape recorders - under his family name for the professional market, and for home use starting in 1951 under the name Revox. In the late 1960s, additional hi-fi components were added as the company gradually conquered the entire audio system equipment market. In 1983 Revox introduced the world's first multi-room system, while in 1988 the latest tape deck series was launched. As opposed to the former tape decks, which sported a technical by featuring various controls, the current products are contemporary, stylish, and understated.

» Combination of high-end technology and design «

PHOTOS: REVOX

Alfredo Häberli Design Development

The concept of the drinking glass series "Essence, Littala" was to combine tradition and modernity and to strike a balance between festive and everyday use and between single and multiple uses.

"Take a line for a walk, Moroso" - The wingback chair is based on the realization that a great deal can be said with only a few strokes. The result was an easy chair with an integrated footrest, which can be used while wearing shoes or not.

» Swiss design creates plenty from as little as possible; at the same time intelligence and innovation always play a key role. «

With its padded surfaces and warm timber, the four-legged chair " Aki Chair," resembles a leaf with its main vein. Aki is Japanese for autumn and the chair symbolically presents this shape.

The Alfredo Häberli Design Development company, located in Zurich's Seefeld-quarter, currently employs four staff members who work on the development of furniture and home accessories. In addition, the company implements exhibitions and handles the interior design of stores and restaurants.

PHOTOS: COURTESY OF THE MANUFACTURERS

Alexis Georgacopoulos Industrial Design

"CMYK" trays are a series of steel table trays. Each of the products displays one of four basic colors of the CMYK-color-spectrum.
Designed in the year 2010, the "Blow" (with the french company ENO) bowls feature a range of glass bowls of different sizes and forms. A special feature is the red rope that serves as a handle and contrasts with the transparent and purist body of the bowl.
"Garden Party" is a serving trolley that was developed as a prototype for Veuve-Clicquot. Its form of a wheelbarrow and loud colors give it the appearance of a children's toy and give it a surpising presence.

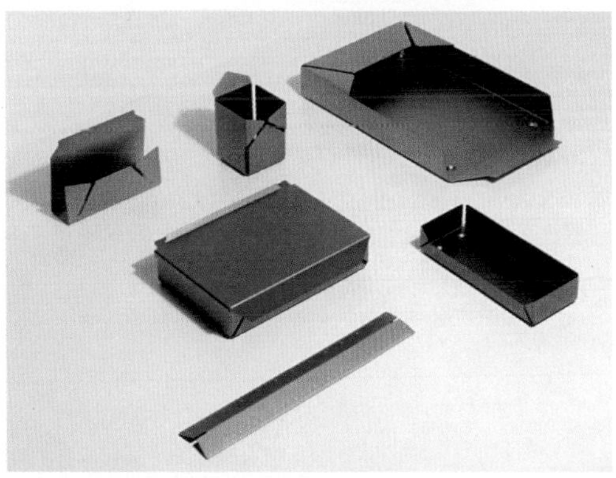

In his work, Alexis Georgacopoulos creates design that both functional and amusing, with humor as the counterweight to technology. His works have been exhibited in major cities, design fairs and museums, such as the Milan Furniture Fair, the London Design Museum, and the Shanghai MOCA, as well as being published in various exhibition catalogues and books. Pleasure, play and classicism - this could be Alexis Georgacopoulos' credo that combines conceptual lightness with simple functions and straight-to-the-point effectiveness.

» Work hard, play harder! «

PHOTOS: COURTESY OF THE DESIGNER

Thorens

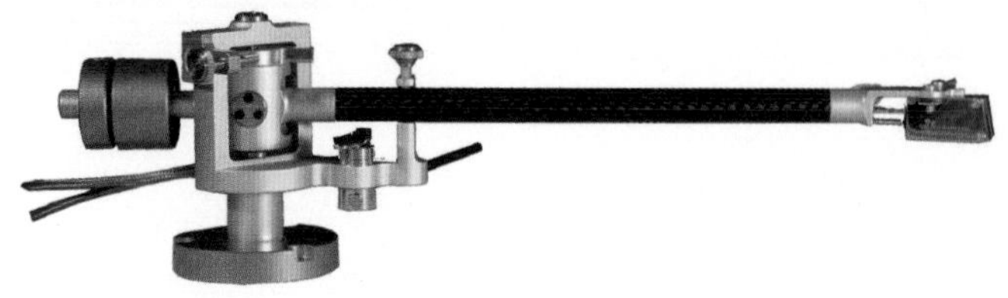

Today Thorens manufactures other hi fi equipment in addition to turntables. The current turntables benefit from the manufacturer's many decades of experience in producing resonance-absorbing and stable housings, evenly operating drives and reliable magnetic cartridges. This is based on the use of select materials, including full timber, acrylic, fused quartz glass, MDF, and aluminum for the body, while veneer, chrome and piano lacquer are used for the surface finish. The product range includes basic models with a focus on sound reproduction, products in the medium price range, as well as, in line with the brand's tradition, the high-end segment.

» Always focus on the essential. «

The history of Thorens began in 1883 when Hermann Thorens of Sainte-Croix established a family business for the manufacturing of musical boxes and clock movements. In 1898, Thorens introduced the first cylinder phonograph and in 1906 the first horn-gramophone for shellac records. At the same time, the company also manufactured harmonicas, cigarette lighters and mechanical razors. In 1927 the family business was changed into a shareholding firm, which in 1928 patented the first electric motor (direct drive) for gramophones. To this day, this manufacturer of high-end audio equipment is known for high-quality stylish turntables. Following a crisis caused by the introduction of CDs in the 1990s, Thorens turntables were able to once again establish themselves on the diminished market.

PHOTOS: COUTESY OF THORENS EXPORT COMPANY LTD.

Zena

The "Rex" vegetable economy peeler, whose design was internationally protected in 1947, is a classic vegetable peeler. With its typical U-shaped aluminum stripe, it was included in a 2004 postage stamp series about Swiss design. It consists of a tempered, polished and pivoted steel blade that is attached to an aluminum handle. The shape is concave at some points, resulting in the required rigidity, while thumb and forefinger fit naturally into the two grooves. The U is held in place by a riveted aluminum axle. The movable knife is balanced by two holes. Two steel sheet clips prevent the blade from turning and position it in such a way that it can make safely make contact with the vegetables.

In the year 1931 Alfred Neweczerzal bought his first punching machine. Initially, he produced various kitchen utensils, such as mayonnaise and cream beaters, along with toys in the basement of a residential home in Zurich. In 1936 he patented a vegetable slicer with an adjustable knife in Germany. The company was entered into the trade register in 1945 and in 1969 turned into a corporation as an individual company. Today, ZENA AG mainly manufactures complete peelers in addition to punched parts, while also offering peeler blades as semi-finished products. Roughly 60 percent of its production volume is exported.

» A design classic usually does not start out as such. «

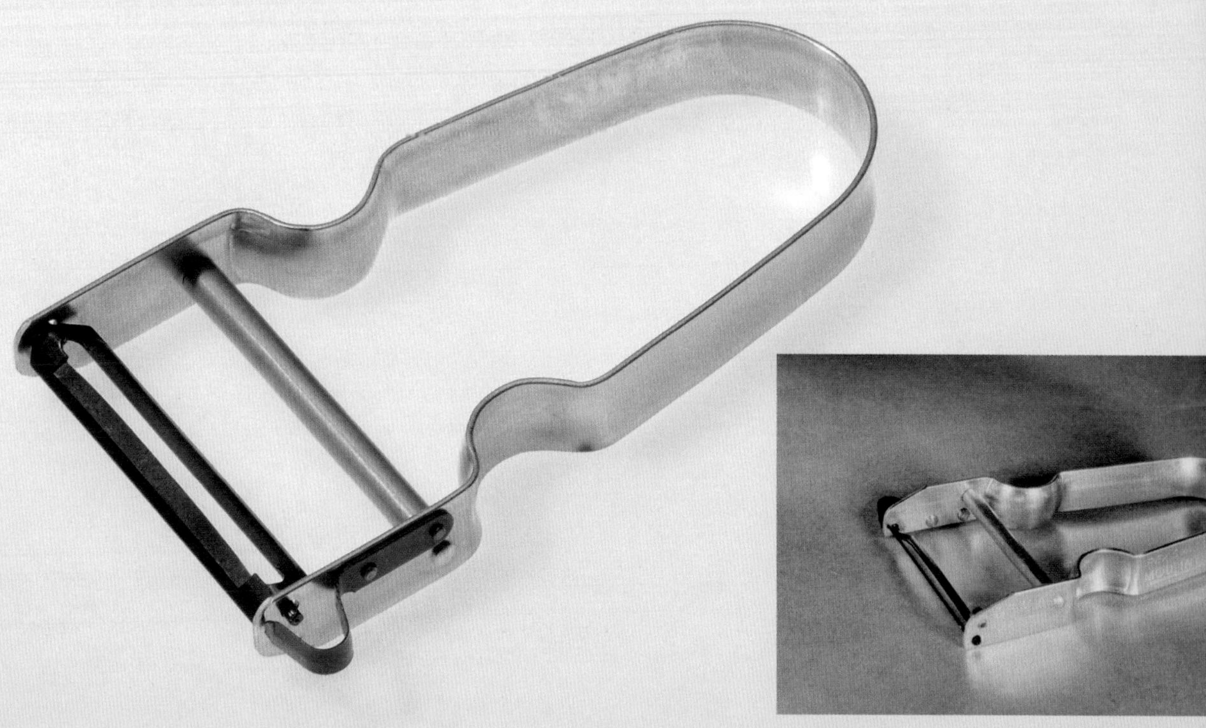

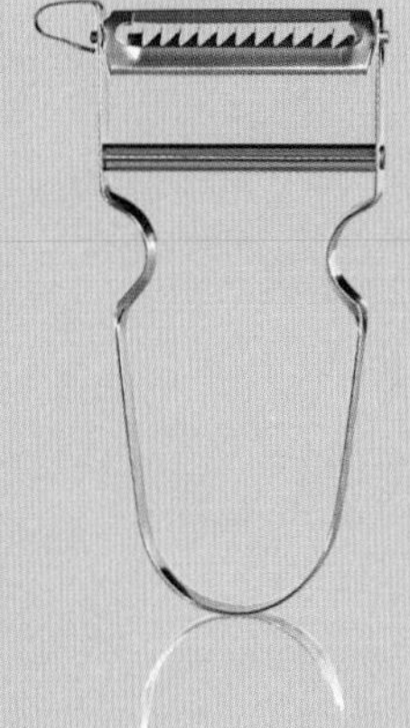

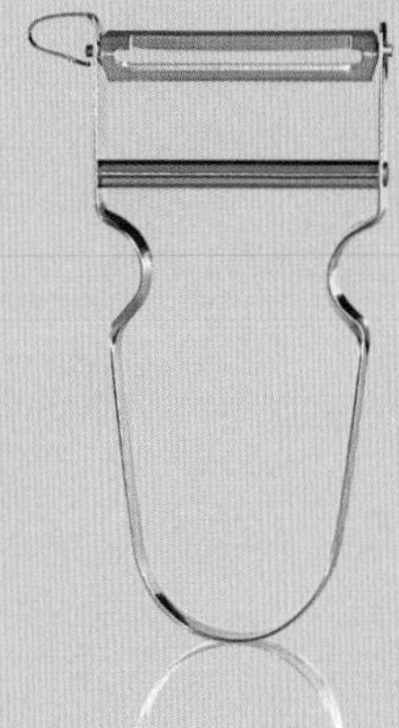

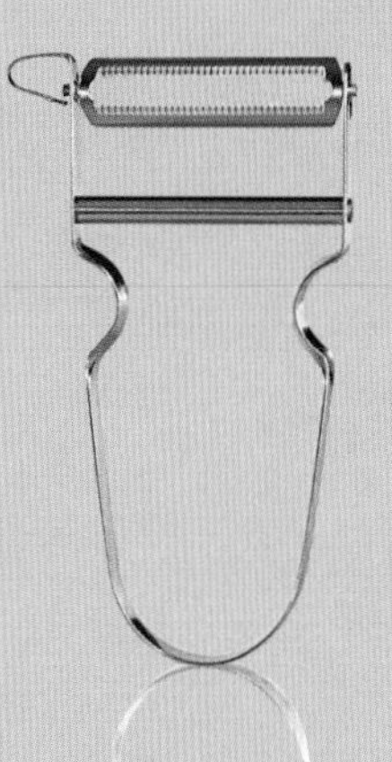

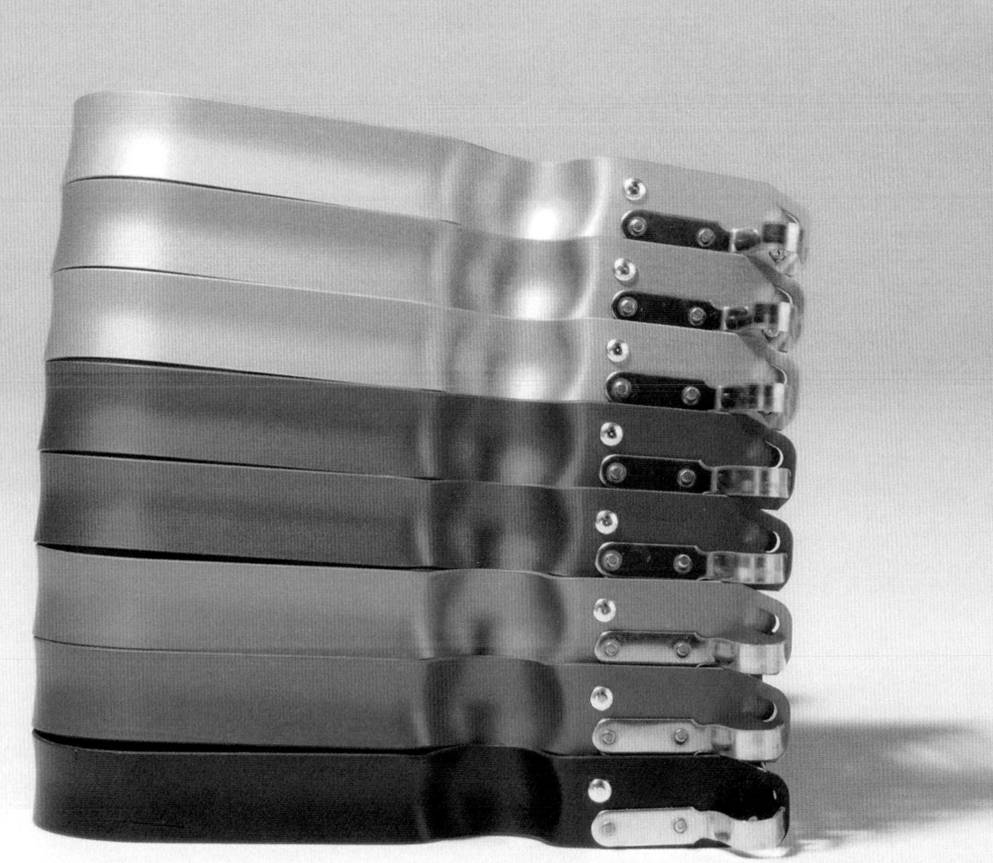

PHOTOS: COURTESY OF THE DESIGNER

David Bernet

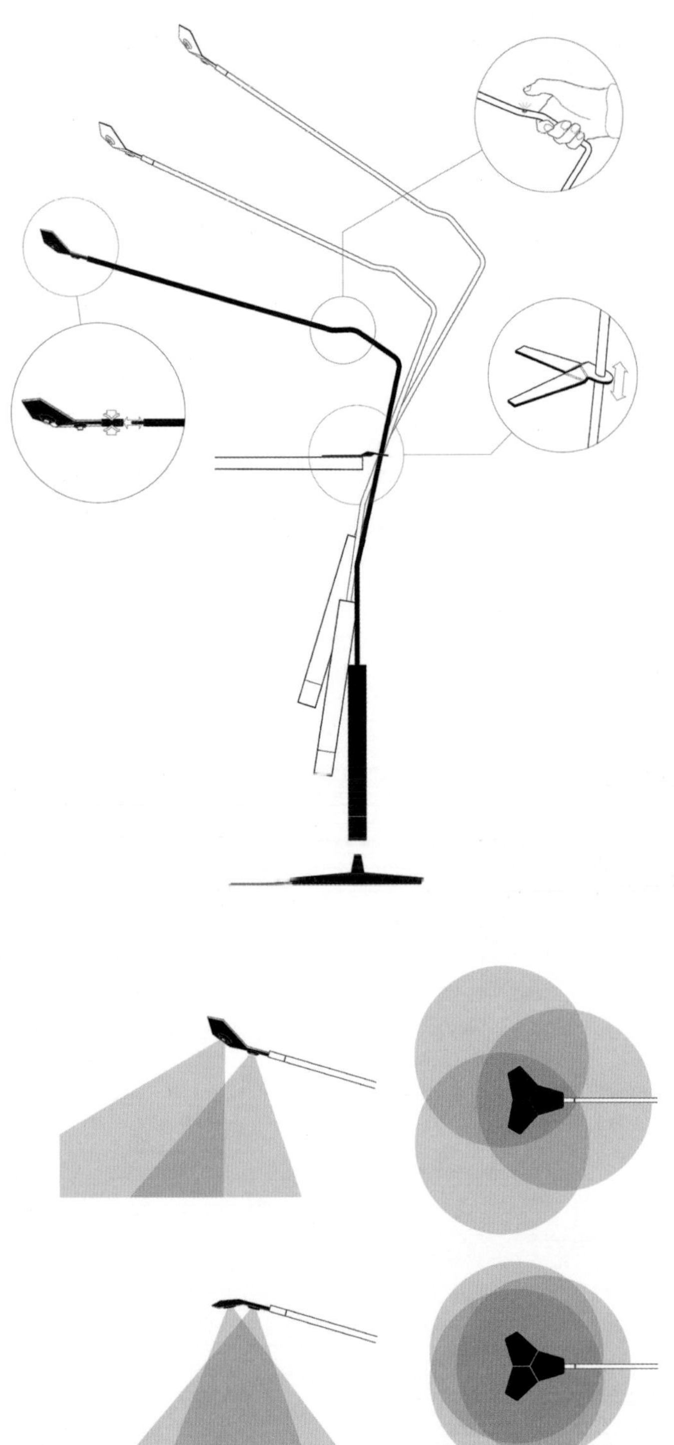

Light is useful for activities such as reading and working, and even necessary during darkness. Every type of activity needs a different type of illumination, light sources and lamps. Reading a book in an easy chair is not the same as writing a letter at the desk. How must a lamp be designed that supports different activities and operates in various settings? Through its rechargeable battery technology and a simple suspension system, the "9,81" lamp is universally applicable and mobile. The LED technology enables a compact structure and extended operation during each charge cycle. The simple click system of the lamp shade allows adjusting the focus of the light at will.

» Compared to other light sources, LEDs have almost no volume, as a designer this provides me with entirely new design options.

David Bernet works as an independent designer under the label db designs. From product design via corporate design up to animations, he offers sophisticated, creative, and customer-oriented design solutions. In 2009 he was nominated for the Swiss Design Award.

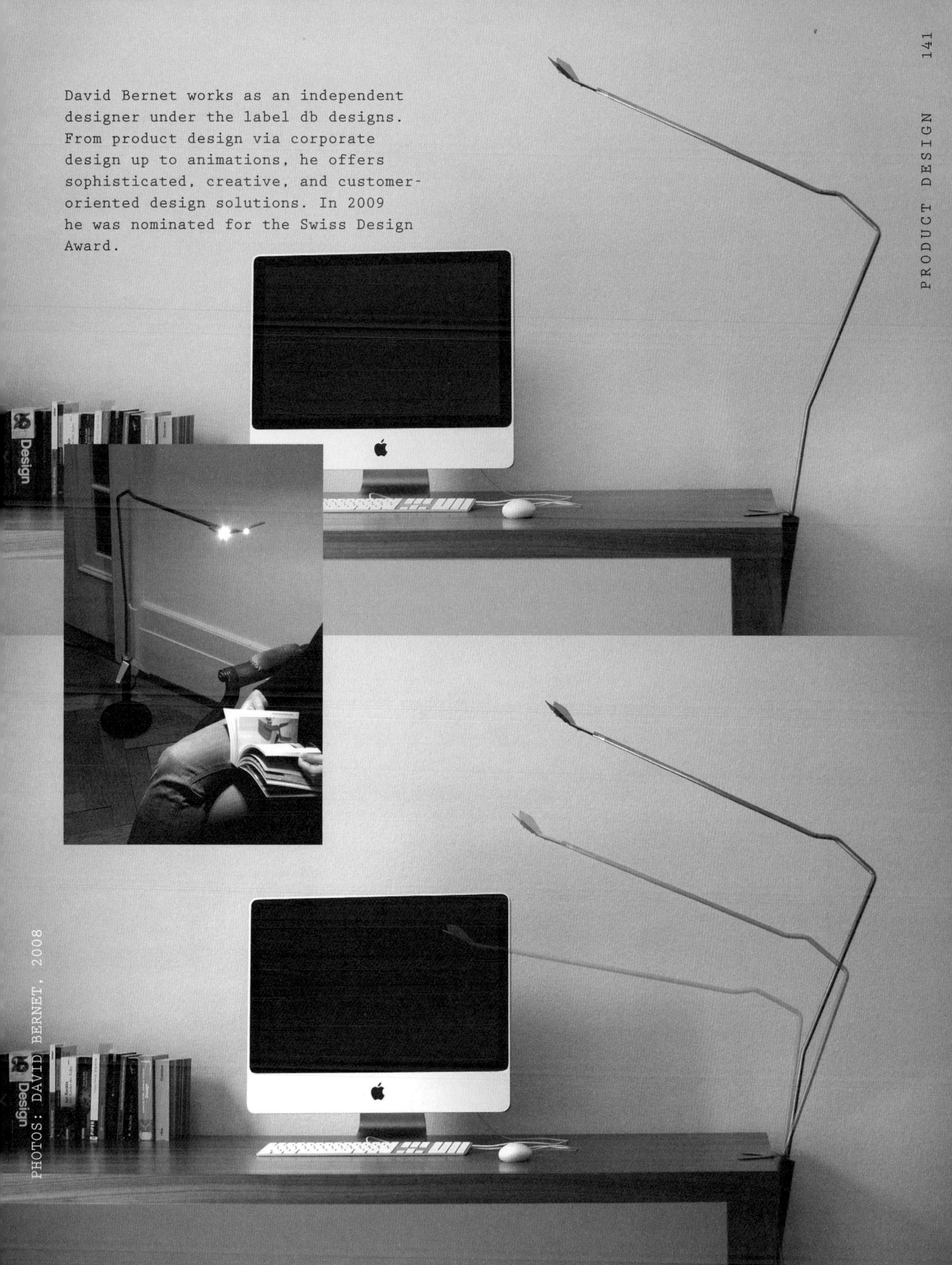

PHOTOS: DAVID BERNET, 2008

Belux

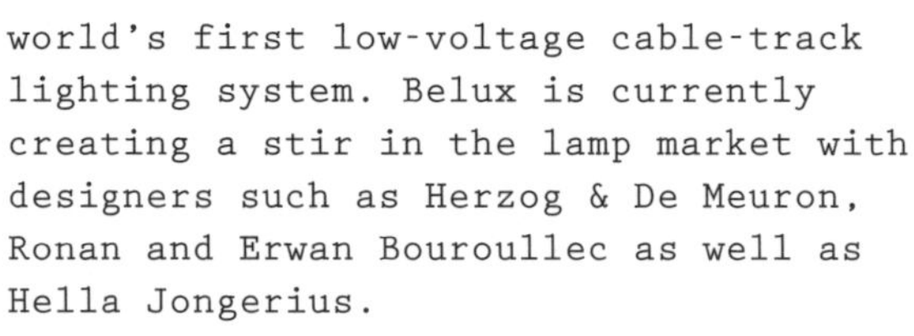

Belux was established in 1970 by Thomas Egloff as a sales company for high quality lamps. However, it soon developed into a manufacturer of elegantly designed lamps of the highest quality. Belux's products are based on innovative lighting solutions and pioneering lamp concepts that are developed in close cooperation with internationally renowned designers and architects. In the late 1970s Belux established a successful cooperation with Hannes Wettstein, with whom it achieved a large break-through in 1982 with the joint development of "Metro", the world's first low-voltage cable-track lighting system. Belux is currently creating a stir in the lamp market with designers such as Herzog & De Meuron, Ronan and Erwan Bouroullec as well as Hella Jongerius.

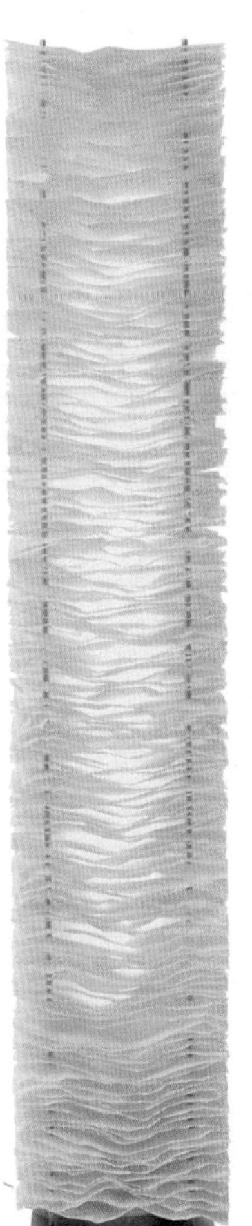

The fluorescent tube lamp "Updown" (designed by Reto Schöpfer) is typical of Belux's combination of form and function. It offers a flowing transition from direct to indirect lighting, while wall/ceiling versions can be equipped with various diffusers and reflectors, adding to the variety of created atmospheres. "One by One" (Steve Lechot) derives its charm from the contrast of stainless steel and fluorescent tubes with the organic pliability of its polyester fleece layers. In the design of "Cloud" (Frank O. Gehry), the same surface material is intended to inspire users to reshape the lampshade while its poetic associative basic shape remains intact. In "Arba" (Matteo Thun), however, the focus is on the archetypical shape associated with local oak as the material of choice.

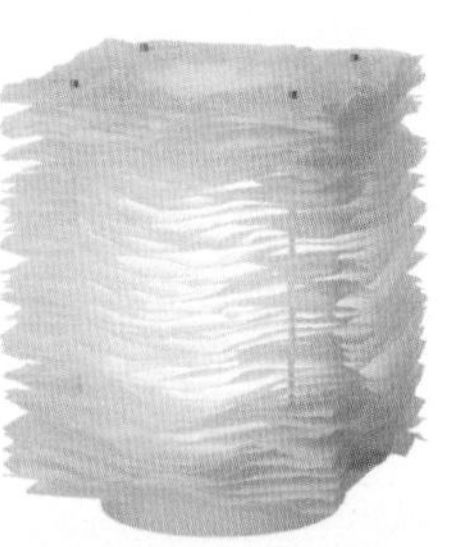

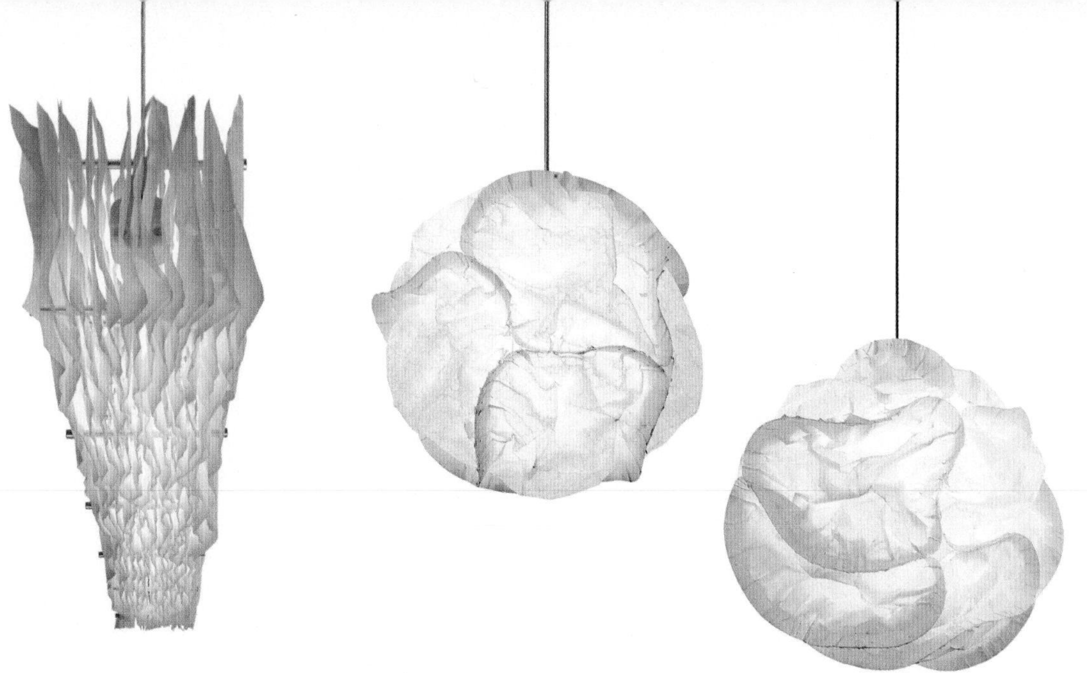

» The combination of light quality, impression and economy «

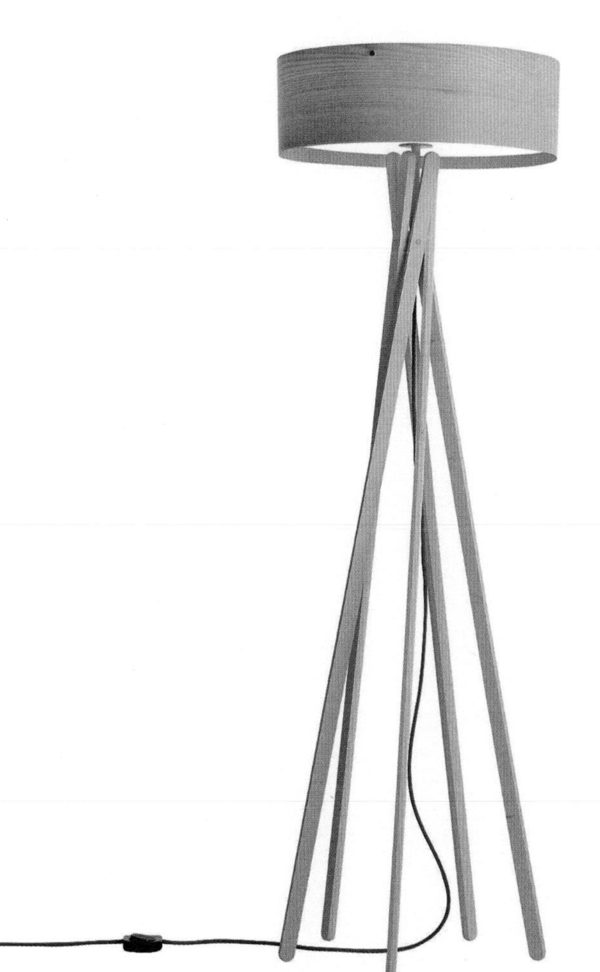

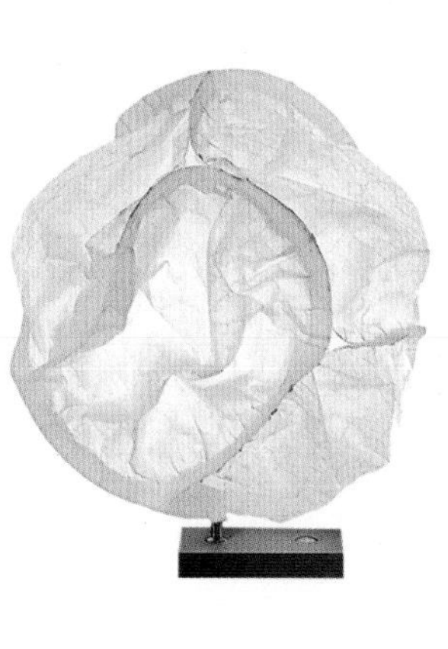

PHOTOS: COURTESY OF THE DESIGNER

Vito Noto

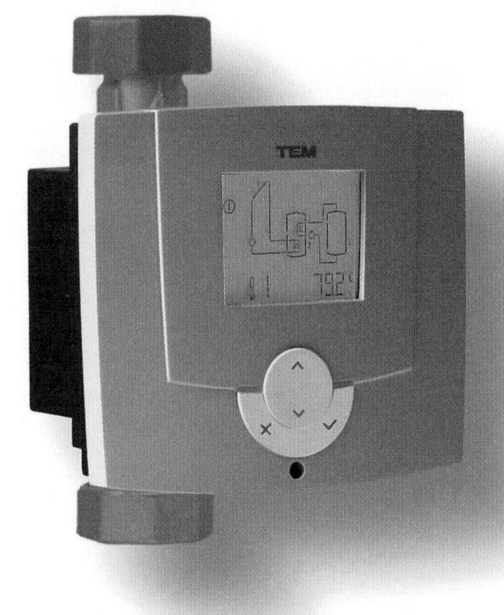

The simple rounded shape of the bottle cooler “GLOBUS Jelo” resembles a fortune-teller’s crystal ball. Compared to its metallic counterparts, this champagne cooler is distinguished by the fact that the cooler, including the bottle and the ice turns into a decorative table sculpture.

The sharpener “TETRAEDRO” is not only a useful office utensil but at the same time a decorative desk accessory. Shaped like a small pyramid with a softly curved outline, its functional parts are hidden behind its smooth exterior.

The wrist watch “GIORNO-NOTTE” combines understated design with surprising technology. The simple chronograph contains a 24-hour display.

For Vito Noto and the specialists included in the various projects, designs must not be merely “beautiful.” A project is only completed once the final product presents a harmonious unit of esthetics, functionality, innovation and economic efficiency. The development process involves knowledge of the application of latest technologies, as well as ergonomic, ecologic, social and psychological aspects, requiring close cooperation between the client and the designer.

» Design is an obligation ... «

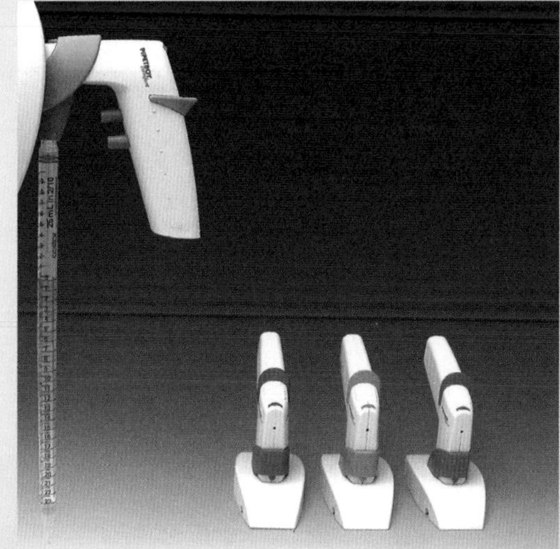

PHOTOS: VITO NOTO DESIGN; LEFT: BY THE MANUFACTURER

Luc Swen

The "Carbon Cradle" is a unique basket made of carbon fiber. It is also an encounter of high-technology and craftsmanship. The design is that of a traditional basket cradle made of most modern materials.
The "Tangram Sofa" is composed of seven parts whose geometric origin is a square, with the four base modules and the three back modules linked by wooden U-shaped components under the sofa. It is a modular sofa system that can be arranged in the most diverse ways.
The watch "Champs Elysees" is made of white gold and Chinese lacquer. It has a mirror polished steel dial, set with 36 diamonds and coupled with a one way mirror allowing a plunging reflection that gives an illusion of a well of diamonds.

» Design is to imagine within space and time. «

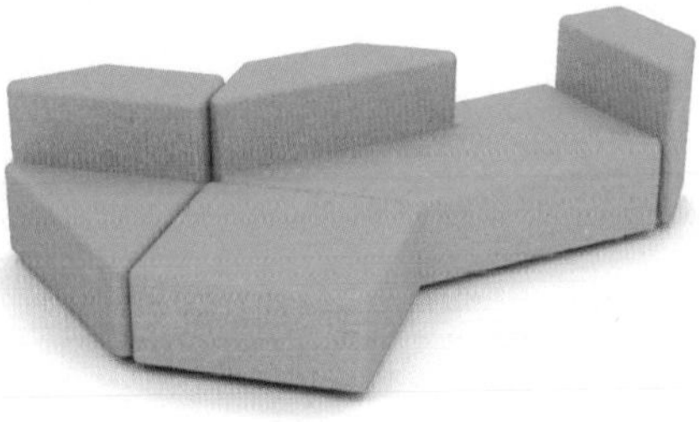

Luc Swen is a freelance design label created by Julien Bernard in 2008. The label specializes luxury product design and 3D rendering pictures. Luc Swen also produces some limited editions in collaboration with the best local artisans while maintaining a certain exclusivity.

PHOTOS: MICHEL BONVIN ECAL 2009

Philipp Gilgen
Industrial Designer

When designing products, the focus and interest of Philipp Gilgen is on their implicitness. This primarily stems from the optimal balance of simplicity and complexity, as reduced as possible and as complex as necessary. Some of his work was published in design books and received several design awards, including the design award of the Bundesamt für Kultur (Swiss national cultural department) and the iF Award.

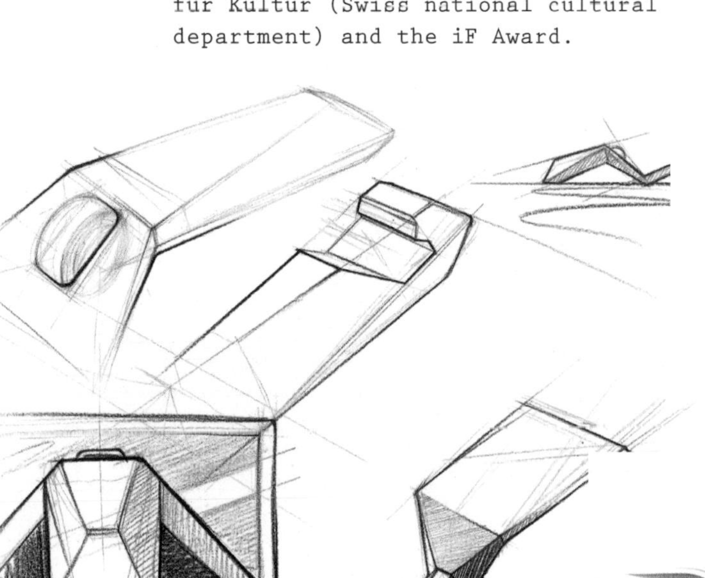

“Coo.Boo” is a digital cookbook whose shape is inspired by typical standard kitchen utensils. Resembling a ladle, it rests comfortably in the hand or on the kitchen counter or is suspended next to dippers and beaters on the wall. The recipes are automatically synchronized wirelessly to the computer.

"Urban Bike Helmet" is a bicycle helmet for everyday use, which one does not mind wearing with a suit or cocktail dress to ride to work or a party. The adjustable ventilation system offers the wearer optimal comfort in rain or shine.

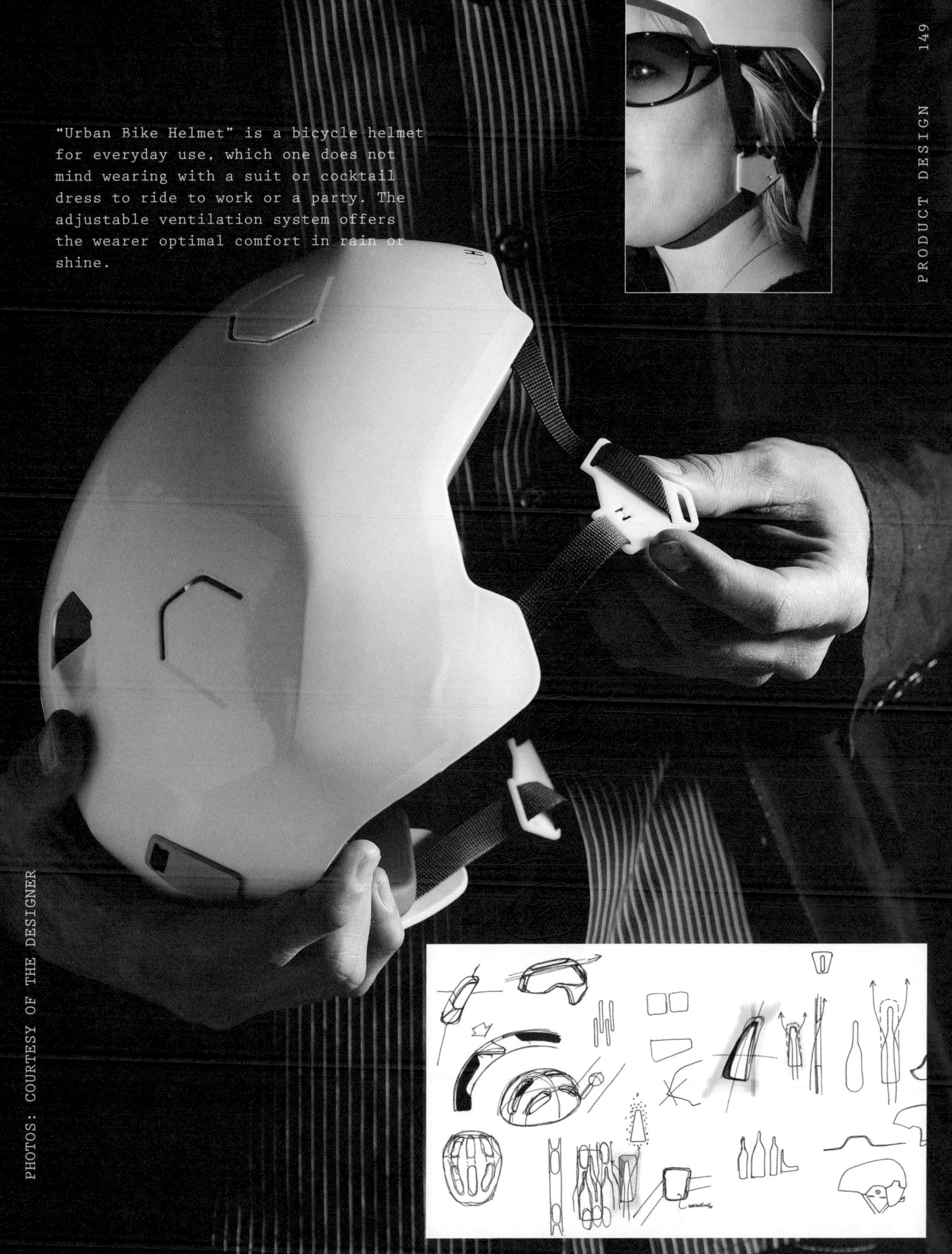

PHOTOS: COURTESY OF THE DESIGNER

Florian Kräutli

This carpet contains integrated, conducting silver threads. The body of the person stepping on it operates as an antenna. The carpet receives radio waves via the body and transmits them to an amplifier that makes them audible.

"For the Birds" are lamp shades made of tapioca, vegetables and wafers. If one does not want to keep them in the house any longer, they can be taken outside and suspended from a tree where they are soon eaten by animals.
"Magnetic Curtain" can be modeled at will. The integrated facetted structure and magnets allow it to keep its shape when pushed up, pulled to the side or pulled down.

The designer likes to observe transformations in both physical and metaphysical contexts. The change of an amorphous material into a structured shape, the shift of values and rituals in daily lives, and recent developments in technology are areas from which he draws inspiration. Florian Kräutli attempts to keep up with contemporary changes and retain a critical view on how they affect our lives and in the potential ways in which they could be used or misused. It is important for him, when diving into a subject, to get a deep insight to communicate the core essence in a simple way to the outside and make it tangible.

» Being outside of Switzerland makes me a Swiss designer. «

PHOTOS: FLORIAN KRÄUTLI. LEFT MID: VINCENT VAN GURP.

Kueng Caputo

At the "cardboard hotel," guests choose their rooms at the reception, based on models. A hole at the bottom of the model provides a look inside and allows them to get a sense of the suite's room atmosphere. The six cardboard boxes can be booked within 72 hours for periods of time ranging from 15 minutes to a full night.

The "Lampada a stelo" was created based on the 'self-made furniture' idea by Enzo Mari, commissioned by the Architecture Association of London. The lamp can be constructed by the buyer based on the assembly instructions.

The "Retired Tennis Balls" emerged from the "Copy by Kueng-Caputo" project. The attempt to copy an original served as a creative inspiration.

Sarah Kueng and Lovis Caputo live and work in Zurich. They began their collaboration in 2006 and graduated in product design at the Hochschule für Gestaltung Zürich. Under the name of Kueng Caputo, their work proposes an ironic and playful approach to daily life. They have implemented innovative projects, exploring mundane materials and environments to exercise and reflect high design/architectural concepts. Kueng Caputo has been invited to museums, galleries, and design/art fairs worldwide, including venues in Zurich, Basel, Milan, Cape Town, Seoul, Osaka, Tokyo, and New York.

» Life has no rewind button. «

PHOTOS: AKI MÜLLER AND KUENG CAPUTO

Caran d' Ache

The hexagonal shape, a distinctive sign of Caran d'Ache, brings together the physical identification of the pencil with the writing instrument itself. Graphite and color pencils, office products, and writing instruments such as the hexagonal "Ecridor" and "Varius", all adopted the famous shape. It allows the fingers to be positioned precisely on the instrument for a genuinely pleasing writing experience. The "Maison de Haute Ecriture" devotes its passion and rigor to designing and producing exceptional products, devoted to the art of writing and drawing. A classic product is the "Fixpencil", invented by the Geneva-born engineer Carl Schmid - in 1930 it was the first mechanical retractable pencil that was able to accommodate leads with different diameters.

» Designed in Switzerland – manufactured in Switzerland. «

When the Geneva Pencil Factory, founded in 1915, was taken over by Arnold Schweitzer in 1924, he gave it the name of a famous French artist he very much admired, Emmanuel Poiré. Under the pseudonym "Karandash", which is the Russian word for a pencil, Poiré worked as a designer and caricaturist in Paris during the Belle Epoque era. Considered one of the fathers of the comic strip, he was most famous for his "Stories without words" which were reprinted by most of the illustrated newspapers of the time. While Caran d'Ache was primarily active on the local market until the 1990s, it has since expanded its range of business around the world.

PHOTOS: COURTESY OF THE DESIGNER

Nicolas Le Moigne

Aged only 30, Nicolas Le Moigne already has one commercial success to his credit - the "Verso Diverso" watering can (2006), developed while working on his bachelor's degree. This is proof that thinking about everyday objects and how they are used can take on the aspect of a re-design that is functional rather than technological. If the simplicity of Le Moigne's suggestions tended to provoke controversy about urban issues, it is to the credit of this young designer who says he is not looking for the revolutionary in the design but for little changes, the esthetic or functional detail that helps in everyday life.

» Discipline Design «

"ECAL stool" is composed largely of cement and different fibers. Although the material is strong, it was necessary to find a way of rigidifying it further, using folds and reinforcements.

Each duo of stand and vase of the "PODIUM vases" is linked by a common technique of enameled ceramics, and based on a mathematical creative logic. The dimensions of each vase, as well as its shape, have been determined in proportion to the size of the stand, highlighting it.

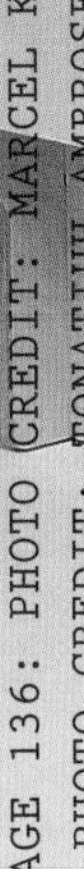

PHOTOS: PAGE 136: PHOTO CREDIT: MARCEL KOCH
PAGE 137: PHOTO CREDIT: TONATIUH AMBROSETTI AND DANIELA DROZ (FOR BOTH PROJECTS)

In the "VESTA tables," wood and steel disguise themselves and become the centerpiece of an exhibition devoted to the duality of art and handicrafts, between highly refined and common objects.

Adrian Weidmann

"LOC+" is a symbiosis of a bicycle light and lock. The lock body is based on the principle of a sturdy U-lock, consisting of a metal ring and a cross bar. The light units are equipped with LEDs and powered by batteries. To use the lock, the front light is detached from the handle bars, and the cross bar removed from the holsters on the back wheel and both are combined into a lock unit. Conversely, the U-lock is unlocked and used as a front light and rear light.

"Horat Mill" is a cruet set consisting of a salt shaker and pepper mill. Large openings with a snap closure allow quick and simple refills. For gastronomy and home use.

Adrian Weidmann has been working since 2006 as an industrial designer and is now based in London. Trained as a machine mechanic and industrial designer, his work skillfully combines technical functionality and attractive design. He designed in collaboration with NOSE, Industrial Facility and Foster + Partners for companies known for their high quality demands such as BMC Cycling, Issey Miyake, MUJI, Established&Sons, LaCie, Ideal Standard, and Louis Poulsen.

PHOTOS: LOC+: PARTICK HAARI ; HORATMILL: DESIGNER

» Swiss design is only underestimated by the Swiss. «

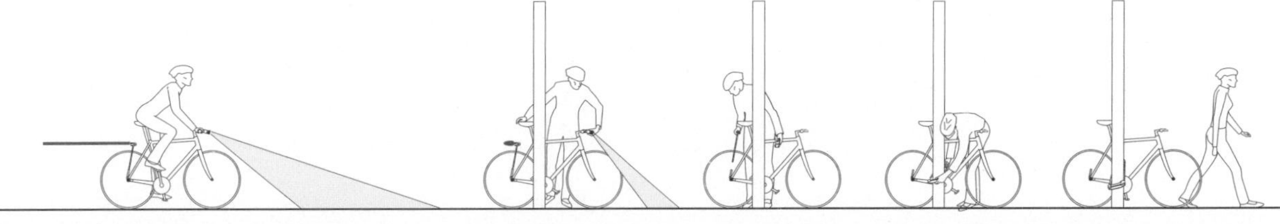

Alex Hochstrasser

"Bilibo" is a multifunctional play object that turns into anything a child wants it to be. Highly acclaimed by childhood learning specialists, the iconic shell is on its way to becoming a new classic, leading a trend back to more simple, sustainable toys.
For the Swiss toy company ACTIVE PEOPLE, Alex Hochstrasser created a large range of skill and motions toys, some designed from scratch, others in collaboration with external inventors. The triple action technology he developed for a new set of yo-yos as well as the stackable ball concept for Babal have been patented.

Having worked and lived in Spain, the United States and Japan, Alex Hochstrasser draws inspiration from many different cultures, merging the Swiss restraint and functionalism with a more playful, experimental approach to design. His work ranges from product development, branding and graphics to photography, video and web design, giving him unique control over a product from the very first idea to when it is finally sold. After early success in furniture and lighting design he has focused mainly on toy design in the last few years, breaking new ground with a family of open-ended play objects.

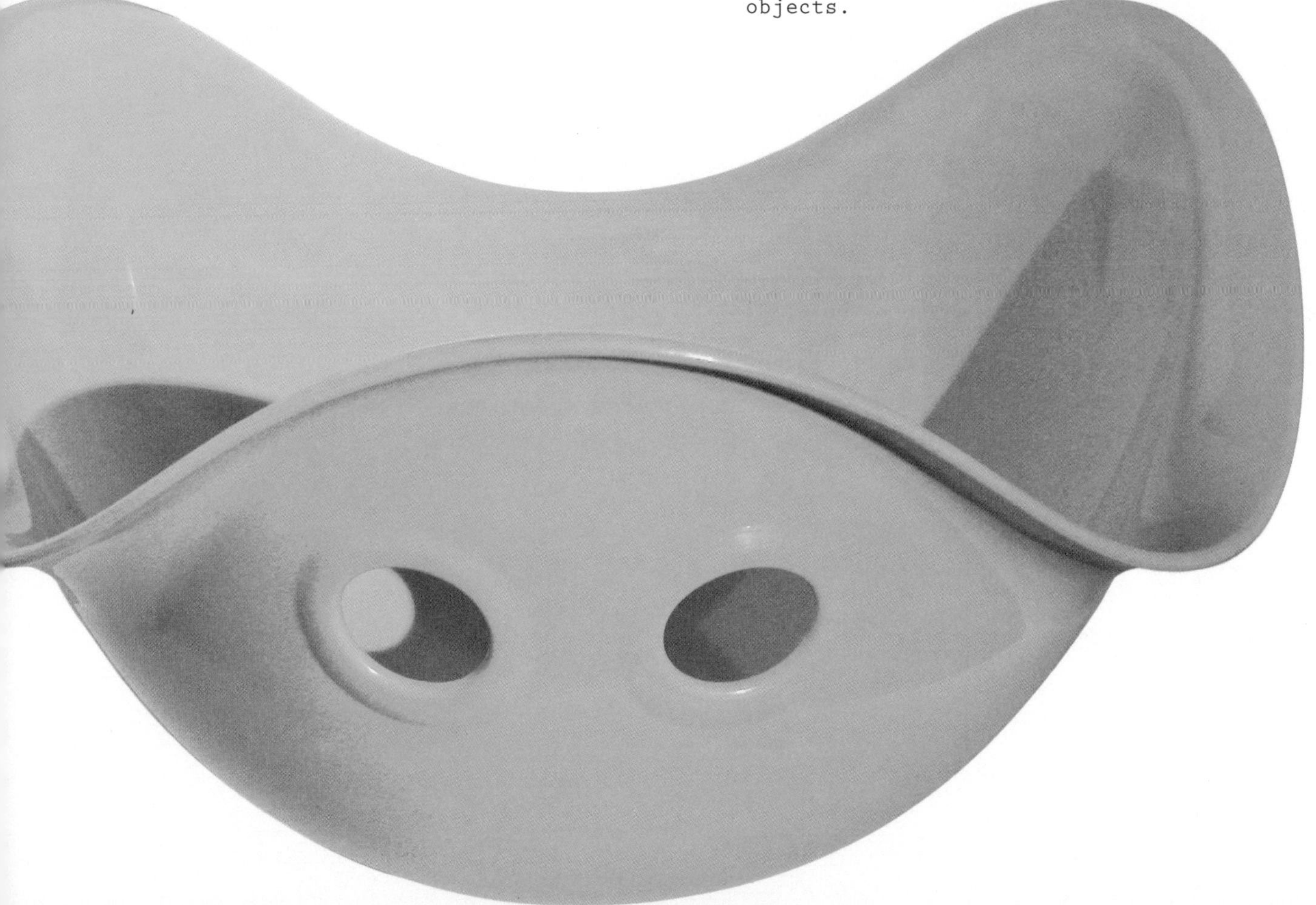

» Good design should put a smile on your face. «

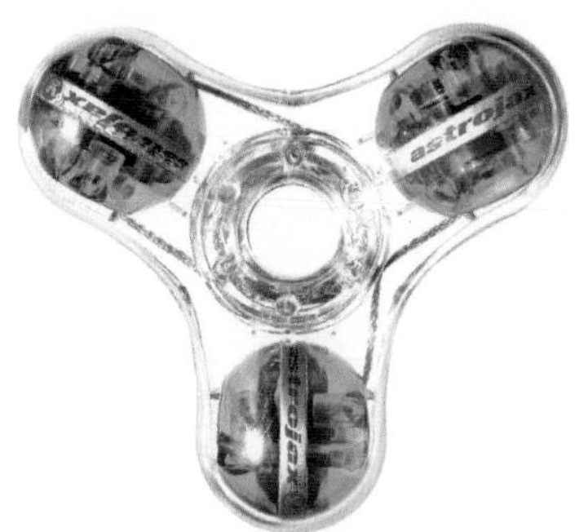

PHOTOS: ALEX HOCHSTRASSER

Sigg

The shape of today's SIGG Bottles is based on hot-water bottles. Their profile is reflected in the classic SIGG "Traveler Bottle", which to this day is the epitome for reusable aluminum drinking bottles. The SIGG Bottle is still constructed from a single piece of pure aluminum. The fact that this eliminates any welding seams guarantees a long lasting and leak proof bottle. Brightly colored, fashionable designs and highly functional caps give each SIGG Bottle its own style. In 1993, it was added to the collection of the Museum of Modern Art in New York. In the same year, SIGG produced the first designer collection, transforming a previous functional product into a fashion accessory and collectors' item.

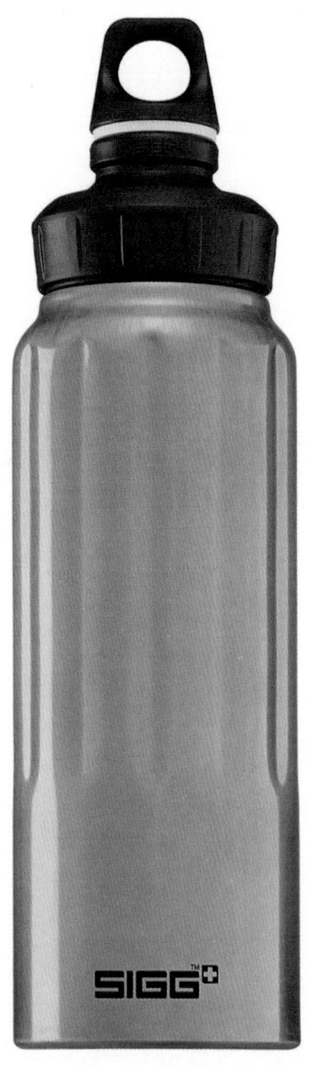

» Fresh and fashionable. «

In October 1908, Ferdinand Sigg and Xaver Küng established an aluminum products factory in Biel. Following a very successful first year, the Küng, Sigg & Co. company flourished and had 30 employees. The product range included cooking pots, frying pans and the bottles that were already sought after at the time. After Xaver Küng left the company, it was renamed in 1917 to SIGG AG Aluminiumwarenfabrik and moved to its new production location in Frauenfeld. In the course of the next eight decades, SIGG sold thousands of household products across Europe and advanced into a prominent brand for everyday items. Within the scope of a strategic repositioning the company focused on the SIGG Bottle exclusively since the year 1999.

PHOTOS: COURTESY OF THE DESIGNER

MTB Cycletech

This bicycle, with the exotic model name "Der Papalagi" is a classic. Produced for the first time 25 years ago, the trekking bike was constantly further developed by designer Butch Gaudy. His latest version recently received the "Hase in Gold" design award by the magazine Hochparterre and Swiss television.

Despite all fashion trends, Gaudy has been working with steel tubing in his bicycle designs for the past 30 years: "Steel is real." This also applies other MTB Cycletech models, such as the "Oxymoron," a cross between a retro-trekking bike and a mountain bike, or his latest creation "Jalopy," a daily use bicycle with a belt drive and disk brakes.

Velobaze AG was founded in 2001 by its owner George Merahtzakis with the purpose of manufacturing high-quality and stylish bicycles suitable for everyday use under the brand name MTB CYCLETECH with a special emphasis on good design. Butch Gaudy exclusively works for the company as its creative director. He achieved fame with the models "Jalopy," "Oxymoron," and "Papalagi." From an early stage, Merahtzakis sought to cooperate with other designers. Together with Jörg Boner he implanted the city bike BAZE and with Hannes Wettstein the revolutionary EST.

» I am fanatical about improving. «

PHOTOS: RETO ANDREOLI, BERN (DER PAPALAGI & OXYMORON), HEIZ UNGER, ZÜRICH(JALOPY)

Zimmerli Design

The design of the fondue set "Mona" aimed to create an elegant fondue chafing dish, which fits naturally into the world of table settings. The primary inspiration came from old soup tureens. The raclette stove "ELSA" shows that design can also be funny. Just like in earlier times cheese was melted on an open fire, "ELSA" melts the topmost layer of the cheese block. Plus, at beginning of every cheese there is a cow. The bed system "Sanapur" consists of aluminum profiles. The insertion frame can be equipped with different spring systems. Set on four legs, the frame even serves as an independent bed.

For more than 30 years, Zimmerli Design has been conceiving products in the areas of home accessories, furniture, electronics, machine construction, and sports. Some of these products have remained successfully on the market for more than 25 years and have received multiple international awards. The to-date most successful product, the SIGG bottle was included in the collection of the Museum of Modern Art in New York. The aim of Zimmerli Design is high utilization quality, simple construction solutions, sustainability, and subsequently unadorned esthetics that remain valid for many years, pleasing their owners.

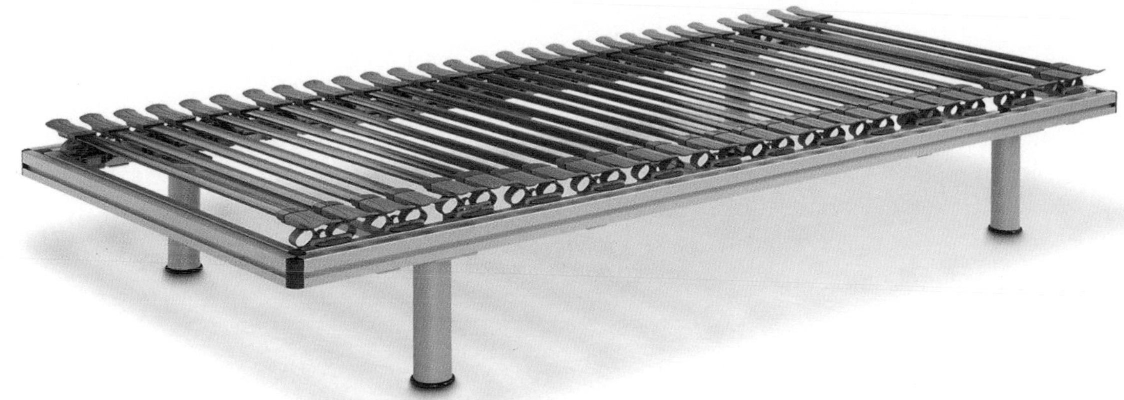

» Well-shaped quality is pleasing — every day. «

PHOTOS: COURTESY OF THE DESIGNER

StauffacherBenz

"Le'mo" is a lightweight electric vehicle for town and local traffic. Due to its low weight, "Le'mo" is extremely energy-efficient, while its innovative technical concept allows it to be produced very cost-effectively even in small numbers. The prototype was developed in collaboration with the Technical University of Rapperswil.

The silhouette of a person relaxing on the grass awakens memories of leisurely weekends and serves as a parking spot for the stressed-out soul of the city dweller during the week. The "Relax!" planter is produced by Eternit.

A contemporary interpretation of the classic drawer table and a staple stool with sculptural qualities were designed for the new furniture collection Atelier Pfister.

StauffacherBenz, studio for product design in Uster/Zurich, was established in 2003 by Nicole Benz and Stefan Stauffacher. Their scope of activities extends from solid classic product design to light-natured playful design statements. StauffacherBenz create a wide range of products, furniture and accessories, jewelry and fair booths. Regardless of whether on assignment by a client or based on own ideas, the designs are innovative while functional, formally precise and technically sophisticated with one aim in mind: spreading pleasure.

» Design from Switzerland is innovative, essential, accurate, (also) modest. «

PHOTOS: E'MO AND ATELIER PFISTER MÖBEL: COURTESY OF THE DESIGNER
RELAX: FOTOS BY JÜRG ZIMMERMANN

Isabel Bürgin

The fashionable floor rug “bastard” consists of 100% wool. Its complex pattern and warm and soft feel even appeal to individuals who prefer reduced styles - a noble unparalleled contrast.
“weichling” (softy) is a 100% wool rug available in 40 colors. It’s all in the name, as its properties can be described as soft, voluminous, and warm. It is a woven “sheepskin” for sitting, lying down, and lolling about - the ideal accessory for urban nomads.
“zicke” is a floor rug made of goat hair. Hairy material meets a surprisingly soft presence and unconventional color combinations - a willful item for original individuals and lateral thinkers.

» The best thing is that every product, no matter how well developed, is imperfect and therefore already contains the core of a new design. «

Isabel Bürgin runs a one-woman business. She constantly develops new products for her own collection, which she has produced in Switzerland and markets herself. Her main focus is on the design of woven fabrics such as floor rugs and woolen blankets. She also works as a freelancer for the industry and has been developing color concepts for fabrics and architecture since 2006. Today, Isabel Bürgin increasingly also develops products in cooperation with other designers, benefiting from the great potential of synergies.

PHOTOS: COURTESY OF THE DESIGNER NIKLAUS BÜRGIN FOTOGRAFIE, BASEL

Tribecraft

"Leggero Vento" is a versatile bike trailer for children with additional space for luggage. Its sporty look is inspired by sailboats. The circumferential tube frame with rollover guard and sturdy aluminum bed provide maximum safety.

The "Monolith" for Geberit redefines the concept of WC cisterns. Water inlet and outlet, flushing tank, controls and mounting are included in one unit. It connects space and ceramics as an architectural element.

"PAC-Car II" is a joint project of ETH Zurich with partners from the industry. Tribecraft contributed to the concept, industrial design and engineering. The car is hydrogen-propelled and holds the world record of the most fuel-efficient vehicle.

Tribecraft specializes in advanced product development: professional skills paired with a passion for brainteasers and the opportunity to make an impact describes the esprit at Tribecraft. A carefully selected team of experts combines diverse educational backgrounds and practical experience in design and engineering. Although Tribecraft works in a broad range of fields like medical, architectural, capital goods and leisure products, the core question of every project is always similar: How can a coherent story be told, how do people interact with what was created?

» La conception suisse: foresighted, fraîche, funktioniert. «

PHOTOS: COURTESY OF THE DESIGNER

Steuri Industrial Design

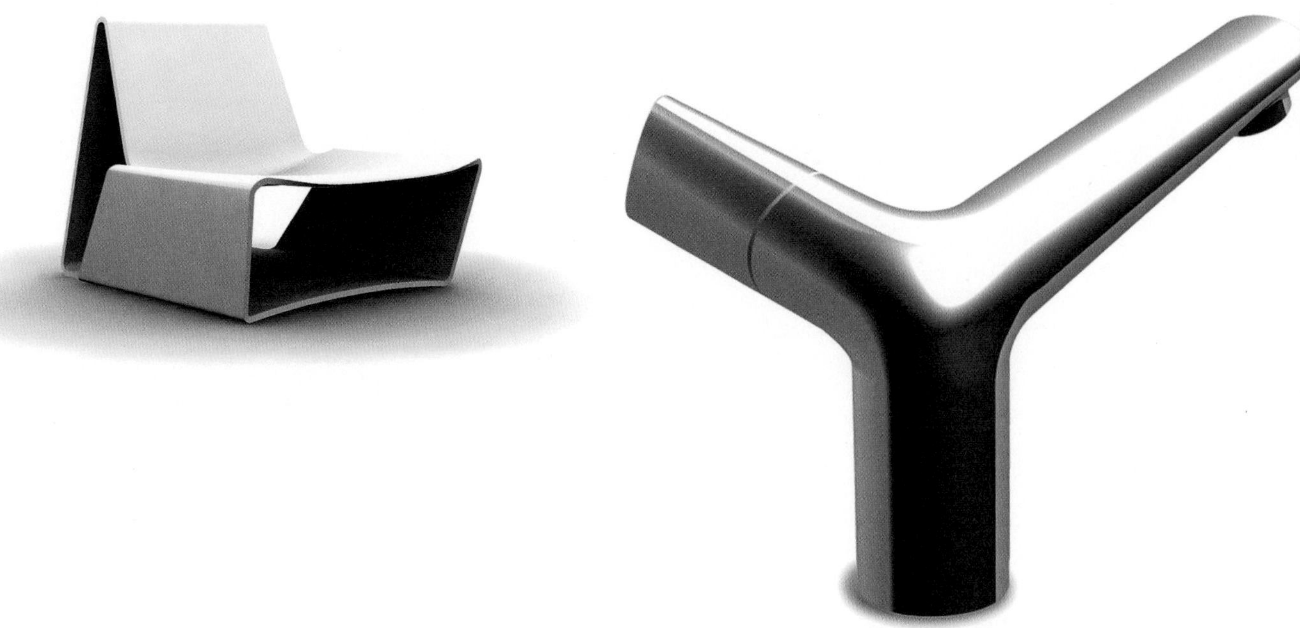

The "DiaScope 85 T* FL" spotting scope of the New Victory DiaScope generation was developed for Carl Zeiss Sports Optics. It is an 85 millimeter scope with a five-lens objective. With a total weight of only 1.45 kilogramm it is barely heavier than a high-performance telescope.
The "elo - washbasin faucet set" is a new concept for single lever faucets that can be made of plastic or metal. The turning handle is integrated almost seamlessly with the faucet body.
The garden furniture range includes high-quality easy chairs made of fiber cement, natural fibers and mineral color pigments. The products, which are hand-crafted in moulds, are robust while also appearing lightweight and

Steuri Industrial Design is committed to excellent design based on the passion for shapes, functions and technologies. Yet not exclusively, as good design is also the result of clear consideration of whom it wants to reach and what it intends to accomplish.
This is why the company favors quality brands. These convey a large degree of credibility, acceptance, and identification potential through their overall esthetic appeal. Steuri Industrial Design is passionate about products whose properties are in line with their esthetics.

» Assigning value to things «

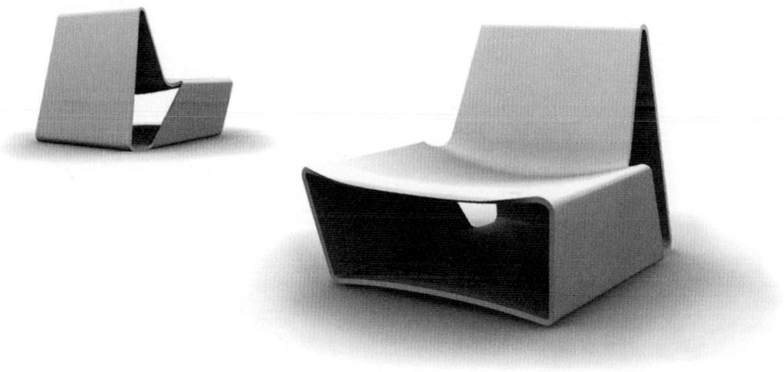

PHOTOS: COURTESY OF THE DESIGNER CARL ZEISS SPORTS OPTICS

CANDIO & BÜTTLER

Developed for Jura, the coffeemaker "ENA" has achieved international success in 2008 and was granted the red dot 2008 award. Available in several colors, its cubic and dynamic shape primarily appeals to a young audience.

"Ginkgo" is a garden chair made of metal. Its shape results from the notched seat, which resembles a Ginkgo leaf. The notch supports the form of the metal sheet and serves as water drainage.

CANDIO & BÜTTLER is a young, Zurich-based studio for architecture and industrial design. From the fully automated coffee maker for the company JURA up to a mansion by the lake, CANDIO & BÜTTLER offers a wide range of projects. The collaboration of industrial designers and architects results in synergies and extensive expertise that can be effectively applied in the development of the broad product range. The consistent guiding theme throughout all projects is to provide a product or a building with a coherent style and a timeless look.

» Basic shapes — powerful expression «

PHOTOS: COURTESY OF THE DESIGNER

dai design

“Arwa-Twinflex” is a sink and washstand faucet with a flexible replaceable hygienic hose that helps save water and energy. In the faucet sector, which is traditionally dominated by chrome steel, the use of new materials and sophisticated technology created a pioneering design with dynamic soft shapes.

“Natural-Sky” is a surface luminary featuring dynamic control of light intensity and a sound-absorbing woven fabric cover. Its new and unique properties make it suitable for use in schools, as well as in the commercial, conference and office sector, as well as for the creation of illuminated walls.

dai is an acronym for design, architecture and identification. To the studio, design is the ideal combination of shape and function that simultaneously conveys the brand identity and values of the customer. This is why it designs and develops products that not only comply with the desired functional and esthetic requirements, but also clearly communicate the corporate identity. With an interdisciplinary team of graphic designers, architects and designers, and with sophisticated solutions that sustainably empower the brand character, dai develops comprehensive concepts for the corporate values of the future.

» Good design has to be simple and impressive. «

Florin Baeriswyl

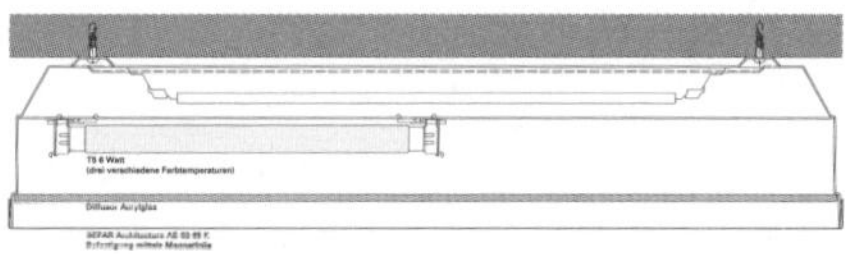

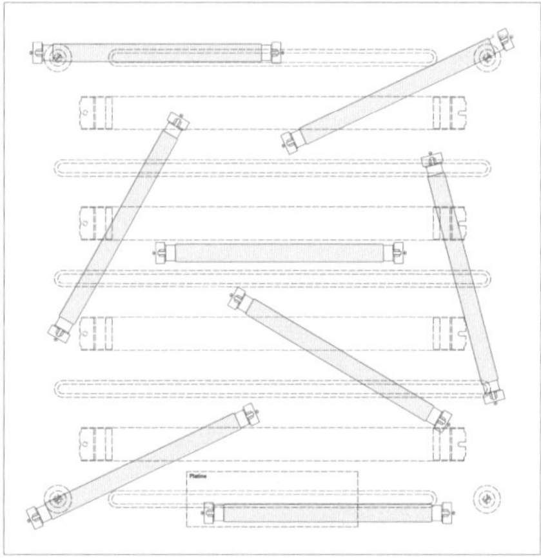

PHOTOS: COURTESY OF THE DESIGNER

» A creative team has the flair to understand the needs of today's customers. «

Bagno Sasso

The reference bathroom of Bagno Sasso is a light-flooded space with a free-standing wooden tub. The faucets feature natural warm, yet light shades of brown. The room's geometry is clearly structured with glass walls that give it an open and expansive character. The special highlight, however, is the floor-to-ceiling exterior glazing and the bathtub positioned in front of it. This offers wellness with a view of the landscape. Whether sitting in the tub with a glass of champagne or sweating in the glazed sauna, nothing obstructs the breath-taking view across the lake.

The Bagno Sasso AG company is headquartered in the canton of Graubünden with subsidiaries in Zurich, Arosa, Landquart and Dubai. The company is active in interior decoration and design with a focus on bathrooms and wellness. In cooperation with internationally renowned designers, Bagno Sasso regularly develops new and independent bathroom products. The noble products received multiple awards such as the internationally coveted "red dot design award best of the best" for the concrete washbasin "Wedge".

PHOTOS: BAGNO SASSO AG

Rigami Design

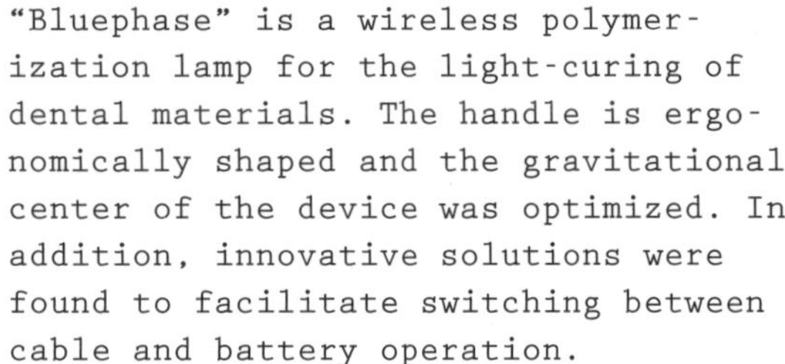

"Bluephase" is a wireless polymerization lamp for the light-curing of dental materials. The handle is ergonomically shaped and the gravitational center of the device was optimized. In addition, innovative solutions were found to facilitate switching between cable and battery operation.
"PULSE Barryvox - Mammut" allows the quick, simple and effective rescue of avalanche victims. In its development, the technology was perfected to ensure simple handling.
The "Zünd digital cutter generation G3" can process a large range of rigid, flexible and foldable materials. These can be cut, chamfered and polished at high speed.

Rigami Design was established in 1992 by Richard Amiel. Since that time, the company has developed and created products with the highest quality, durability and ergonomic properties. The particular strength of Rigami Design is based on its long-term cross-sector experience and its consistent flexibility and speed. Products by Rigami Design received many awards, including the red dot design award and the Volvo Award.

» FORM IS THE PURPOSE OF DESIGN. «

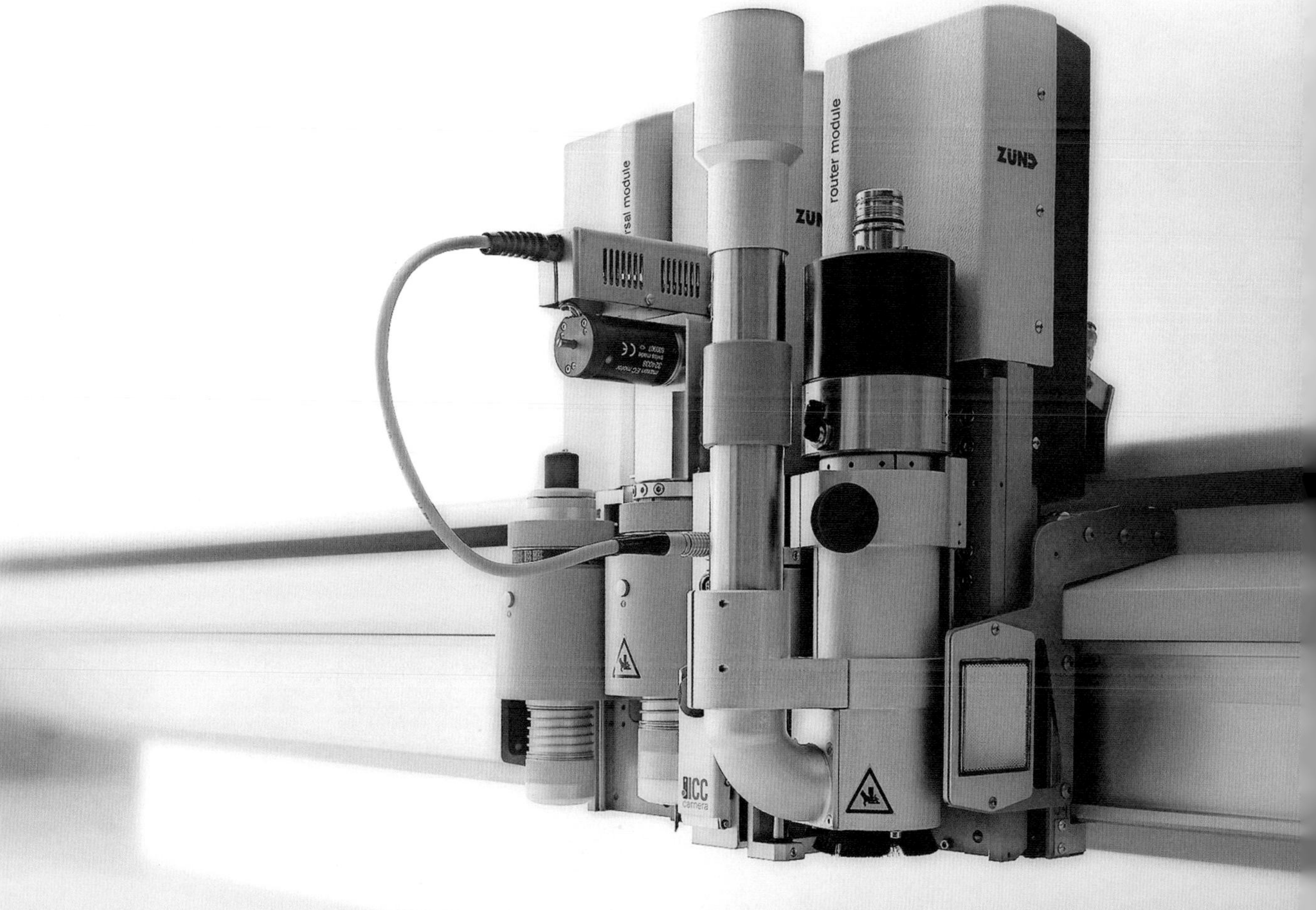

PHOTOS: COPYRIGHT RIGAMI DESIGN. IVOCLAR VIVADENT - BLUEPHASE.
ALEX BAYER - ZUND_G3

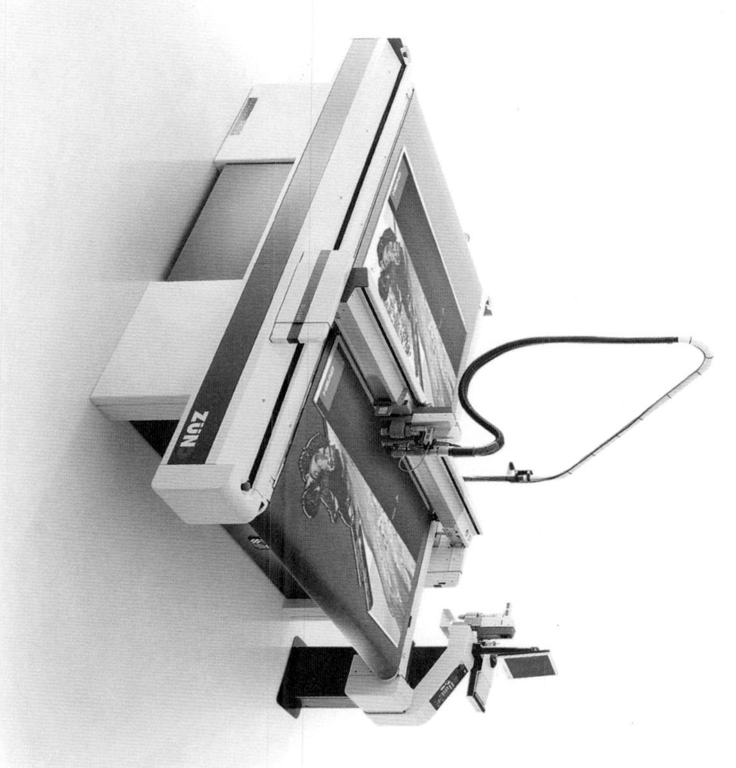

Process

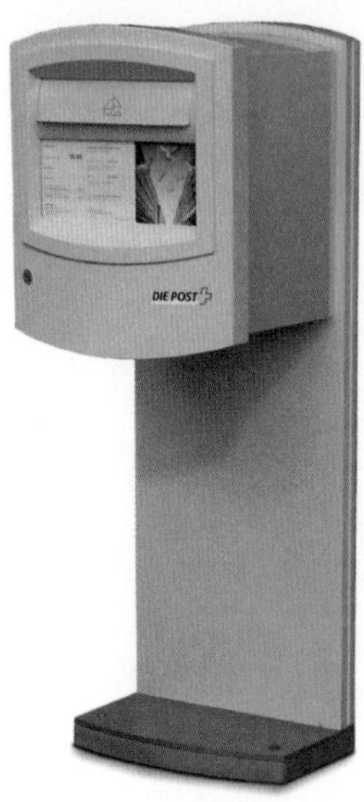

Developed for the demands of Lufthansa, this on-board dinnerware combines simple design with a high degree of practicality. Stability and anti-slip properties were key elements in the development of the items.
The male handbag was developed for Navyboot. The bag is made of smooth leather and is robust and attractive at the same time. The brand name Navyboot was incorporated into the leather.
The Acon light bulb cleverly plays with the shape of its predecessors. The openings of the bulb give it an agile and light look. It is almost too special to be hidden behind lamp shades.

Process, Partner for Brand Excellence, was established in 1995. Today the agency has more than 40 employees at three locations - branding and corporate design in Zurich, and product design in Luzern and Taipei. From branding strategies, up to the complex development of CD programs, from innovation management via usability concepts to sustainable product developments, Process always develops conceptual, consistent and comprehensive brand and product solutions. Process' customers include large and small, international and regional companies.

» Swiss Design is the ideal symbiosis between quality, functionality, esthetics, and fascination. «

PHOTOS: COURTESY OF THE DESIGNER

milani d&c AG

"AAE" - the driving force of railtransport: a visionary concept, innovative impulses and creative ideas developed "AAE" into the leading European company for the rental of standard rail freight cars.

The internal structure is visualized on the covers of the "Bico mattress" - varying functional fabrics, adjusted to the anatomy, support functions and ventilation solutions, demonstrate the functions of the product.

The "Medela nipples" imitate the anatomy of the human nipple - temporary bottle feeding (e.g. for health reasons) does not result in weaning and allows the problem-free return to breast feeding, optimizing the general situation for mothers and babies.

The clarity and surface structure of the "Milk warmer and Sterilizer" signalizes purity and clinical hygiene. The stacking function enables simple transport.

» Complex. Amazingly simple. «

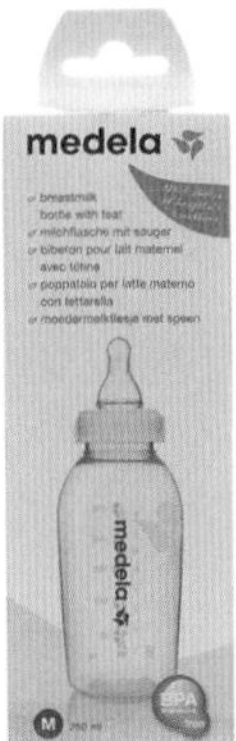

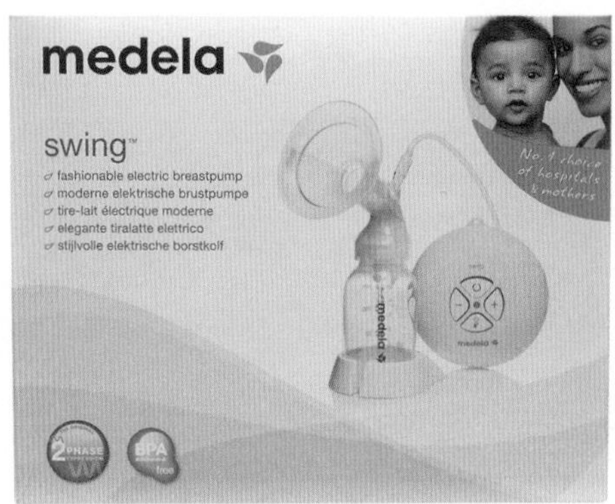

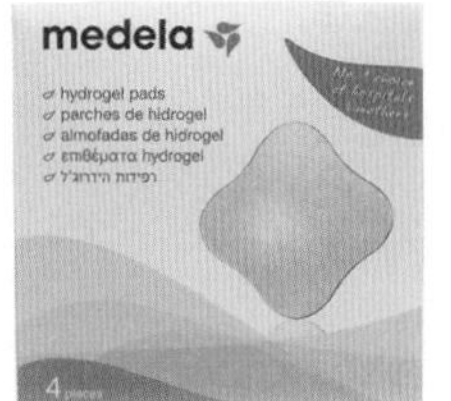

Established in 1963 by Francesco Milani, pioneer of the medical design sector, milani design & consulting AG has evolved into a globally leading agency for highly complex design projects. The agency portfolio extends from pure design via sustainable strategy consulting, to start-ups. Its customer portfolio includes globally leading companies from the medical as well as consumer and investment goods sectors. The penetration of new markets coupled with the development of its own design and consulting modules continuously enhance the expertise of milani.

PHOTOS: COURTESY OF THE DESIGNER. PHOTOS: ERIC SCHMID.

Daniel Gafner

"James" is a tectonic sculpture, side table and shelf all in one. This open structure accommodates different book, magazine and CD formats. It is equal on all sides, and can thus be utilized independently. It is a piece of furniture that can suit the requirements of modern households.

"First Light" is a reading light that is powered by a weight and teethed wheels like a clockwork. The electricity is not derived from the socket, but directly produced in the casing. Sustainability, esthetics and functionality are playfully combined in this object.

Daniel Gafner is a member of the POST-FOSSIL design collective, which produces items for everyday use from environmentally friendly and renewable resources. It develops socially and environmentally friendly designs that are distinguished by their functionality and durability.

» Swiss design is extraordinary, ordinary. «

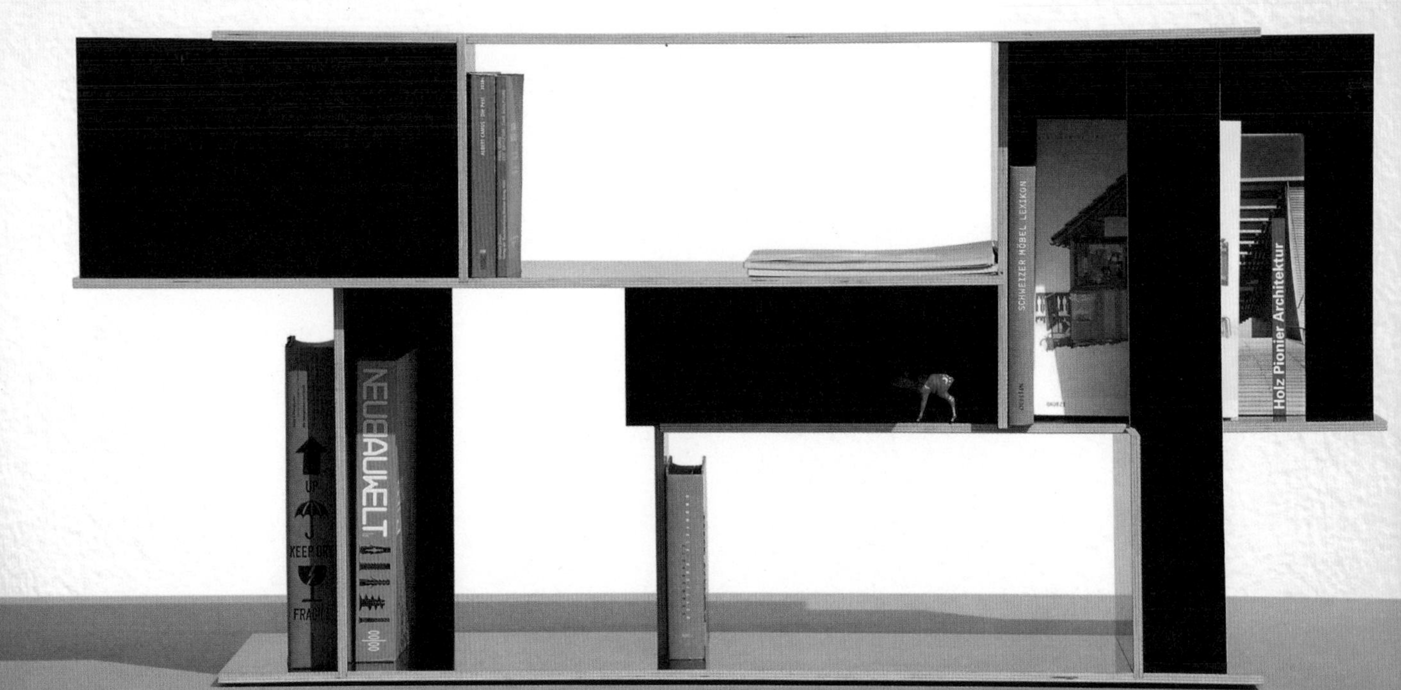

PHOTOS: LEFT: COURTESY OF THE DESIGNER; RIGHT: MIRJAM GRAF, ZÜRICH

TESTA MOTARI Design Manufaktur

To add an emotionally appealing component to perfect technology, the "CRESTRON TPM8X", which is primarily used to control modern yacht and home technology, was provided with select materials that give it a superior feel and look. Yacht owners use the device to control the on-board technology, while home entertainment fans can operate their home cinema system. The handling surfaces are covered in noble hand-sewn nappa leather while polished wenge wood was applied to the front of the device. The docking station and the back were classically enhanced with a polished black piano surface.

Testa Motari is a young and creative label that focuses on exceptional design variations. The products of Testa Motari are distinguished by innovative design, choice materials and high-quality implementation. Testa Motari has implemented a wide scope of design options for very diverse products. The label can offer flexible product solutions from individually crafted items up to small series: The focus is not only on the design of the products, but also on improving the handling and function of the products.

» Making beautiful things even more beautiful! «

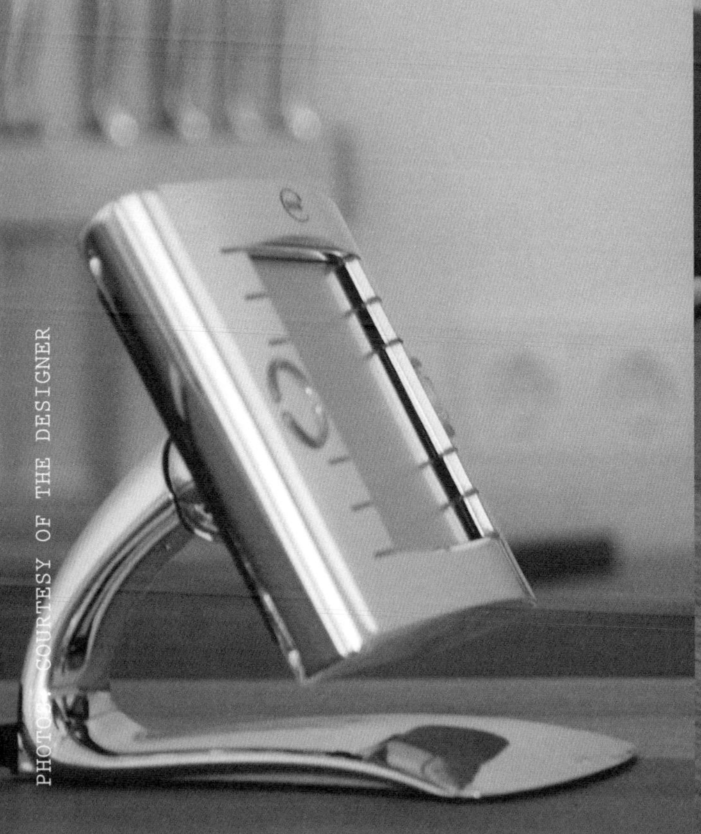

PHOTOS COURTESY OF THE DESIGNER

Meyer-Hayoz Design Engineering Group

The fitness equipment, "premion-line" was developed based on the slogan "Designed for Fitness." The equipment has an innovative and modular design, enabling completely new options for training and fitness studio layouts. "VITA-Systemlösungen" is a firing system for dental ceramics firing, which for the first time allows dentists and laboratories to select their ideal configuration and to control it by means of an icon-oriented touch screen. Additional dental system elements include displays for artificial teeth, containers for dental ceramics as well as the worldwide leading colour selection system "VITA Linearguide 3D-MASTER."

The company supports start-ups, small and medium-sized businesses as well as worldwide leading companies in the areas of innovation development, design research, industrial design, user interface design, usability engineering, brand strategy, temporary architecture and communication design. The Meyer-Hayoz Design Engineering Group is an owner-managed company and is one of the leading design companies worldwide. Its focal areas include medical technology, investment goods and high-profile consumer goods.

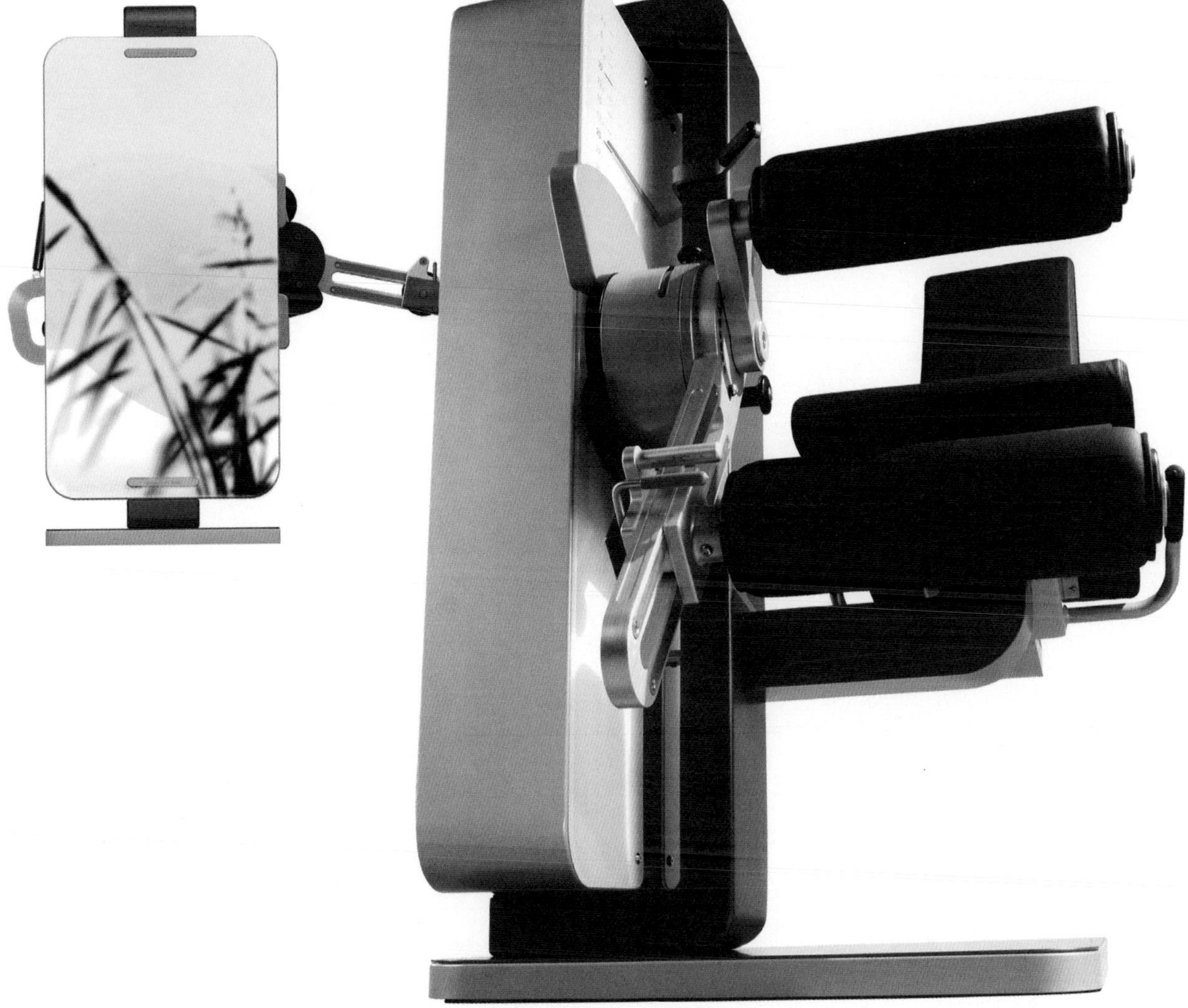

» Design is curiosity and anticipation. «

PHOTOS: COURTESY OF THE DESIGNER

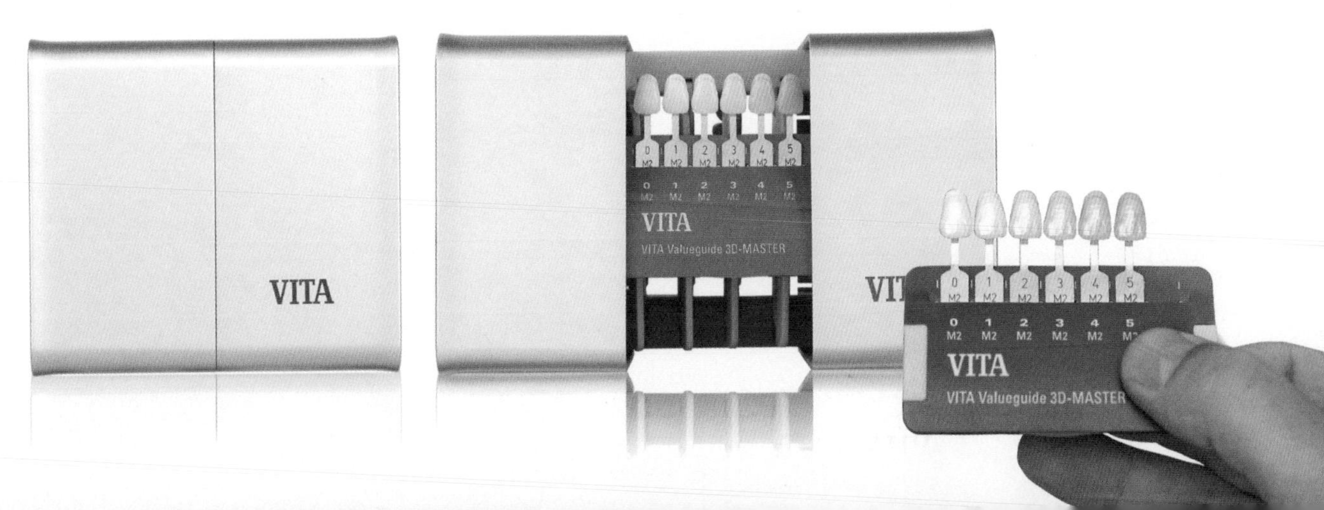

studio thomas blank

A central focus of the designer's work with glass is to question its natural properties such as transparency, luster and a smooth surface and to show a different side of the material. The contrast between the inside and the outside and the different surfaces are the basis of the specific fascination of his objects. Similar to the way potters glaze their material, Thomas Blank attempts to provide his glass bowls with a surface resembling ceramics or metal.

» Glass can have many faces. «

The studio thomas blank is specialized in the production of unique items, small series and prototypes made of glass. Cooperation with other designers promotes the exchange of ideas and expansion of the esthetic range and is therefore always very welcome. Since its establishment, the studio was able to develop extensive specialized knowledge of glass as a material and the possibilities of working with it. Several years of experience and cooperation with various glassworks in Europe and the USA additionally provide him a very useful network.

PHOTOS: COURTESY OF THE DESIGNER

ZMIK | studio for spacial design

"SCHLITTEN" (sled) is the name of a mobile piece of seating furniture that can be pulled like a sled from one location to another. A wooden cube is enclosed in industrial felt that simultaneously serves as a carpet, seating pillow, pulling handle and sliding surface.

"SEVENSISTERS" is foldable display furniture for a designer boutique with a frequently changing line of goods. The system can be adjusted to the constantly changing needs of the boutique. The legs are made of beech wood and the bodies of painted core wood.

» Context & concept, story & smartness «

"BATMAN & ROBIN" is the name of a suspended lamp duo, which is folded from a single piece of an aluminum composite, with a core that serves as a hinge and at the same time lights up the edges.

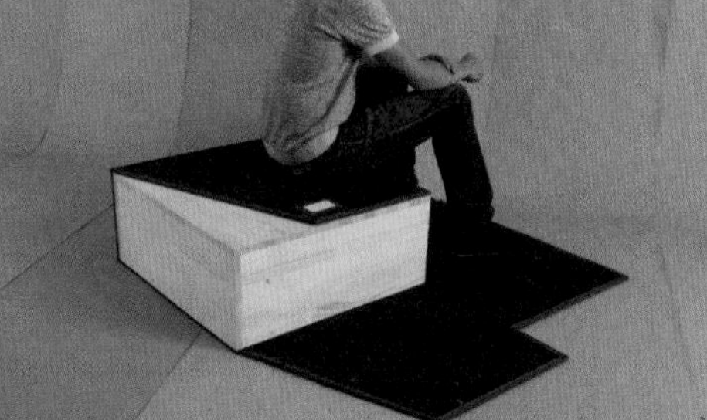

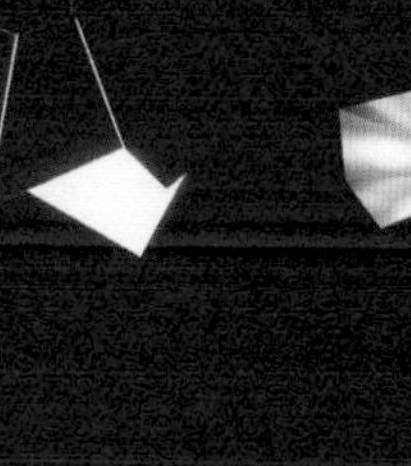

PHOTOS: SEVENSISTERS: TOM BISIG

ZMIK is a studio for spacial design. In the periphery of different disciplines, it develops concepts and strategies within the scope of space and communication. The projects blend architecture, scenography, graphics, media, and object design into self-contained, hybrid and comprehensive spatial concepts. The focus is always on creating identities and individualities and the transfer of abstract contents and messages into spatial settings. ZMIK implements projects in the areas of interior design, architecture, exhibitions, object design and installations.

ARCA-SWISS (International)

The "cube C1" reflects a unity of design and technology. The "C1" is a cube measuring 85x85x100 millimeters, made of a sum of functional elements such as finely embossed swivel mechanisms that spatially move the devices at the center of the swivel arc.
"Misura" is a precision tool that can be carried easily. The object also gracefully complies with an interest in classic photography - large-scale pictures made mobile.
The "Rm3d" is the most modern shift-tilt camera for architectural, industrial and landscape photography. It can be applied either as a hand-held camera or with a tripod for analog and digital photography.

» New Ways, New Realities. «

ARCA-SWISS is an 85-year-old company founded in Zurich with a European subsidiary in France since 1999. Since its founding, ARCA-SWISS both develops and manufactures its products. The company is among the pioneers of the photography sector and has established an excellent reputation and international acclaim with its innovative and high-quality products.

PHOTOS: COURTESY OF THE DESIGNER

brandnewdesign.ch

The heatproof silicon “Bulbcaps” are lampshades that are mounted directly on light bulbs. The caps suit the bulbs like a skirt. Fortunately they also fit the new eco-bulbs in the classical shape, as those really need to be dressed up.
“Fibonacci” is a silicon rubber lampshade. The idea was to design a soft structure that only exhibits a volume when in use. The structure is based on a spiral, which was copied and interlinked into a grid.
The “LostFoam” series is inspired by an aluminum casting technique called lost foam. The designer uses disposed polystyrene-foam packing embedded in sand. The liquid metal is poured into the foam, which disintegrates allowing the foam to be replaced by metal.

Brandnewdesign stands for the possibility of a co-existence between the experimental and the commercial aspects of household products. Since the year 2000 Alain Jost has been practicing his hands-on style of design. Experiments with prototypes are essential, because Alain Jost always keeps an eye on the unexpected and he believes in the

cross-contamination of different ideas. The challenge is the coherence of an object: human behavior, shape, functions and materials must play together in a unique way.

» My most important teachers are Prof. Lazy, Prof. Broke and Prof. Clever. «

PHOTOS: ALAIN JOST

Anna Blattert

The lamps "Sabooh and Mitsu" show that energy saving LED technology can also be used in the home.
Inspired by oriental lanterns, the translucent porcelain shades give off a warm, indirect light. The golden decoration on the inside of the shade serves as a reflector, as well as a conductor from cable to bulb.

With the amulet "treasure or trash" filled with crude oil, a material becomes jewelry that is usually associated with other connotations. This 'misappropriation' begs the question "treasure or trash?" The answer lies in the future.

» As a designer you should have the guts to step out and take a position. «

POSTFOSSIL was established in 2007 as a collective of young designers who conceive and implement objects within the scope of diminishing resources and in anticipation of the post-fossil fuel era.
Environmentally-friendly and resources-conserving creations are the basis with which the collective wants to introduce a new level of sustainable production.

PHOTOS: MIRJAM GRAF (SABOOH & MITSU)

cuboro

The “cuboro” marble track system is made of beech wood cubes with 5 centimeters sides. The elements contain track functions on the surface and the inside and offer an unlimited number of combination possibilities.
“cugolino” offers children aged 3 years and above a thrilling challenge for building and rolling. “cugolino” is 100% compatible with “cuboro” and thus the ideal entry point to the fascinating world of “cuboro”.
“Alhambra” is a didactical jigsaw puzzle in keeping with the puzzle-tradition. Whether as a stimulating instructional game in kindergartens and schools or as a family game, with its twelve geometrical basic elements and altogether over 1300 parts, “Alhambra” offers a broad spectrum of possibilities.

Established in 1997 and based in Haslital/Berner Oberland, the Swiss cuboro AG sells, in addition to high-quality wooden toys such as the “cuboro” and “cugolino” marble track systems, the strategy construction game “babel” and “babel pico”, as well as the jigsaw puzzle game “Alhambra” and Japanese precision marbles. Matthias Etter is the founder of the company and the inventor and designer of “cuboro”, “cugolino”, “Alhambra” and “babel”. New games and concepts for game animations, as well as a didactic learning concept are currently under development.

» Designed to play clever a lifetime. «

PHOTOS: COURTESY OF CUBORO LTD.

RaceGear

» Born to attack. «

The "ScorpionRacer" offers a totally new winter sports experience for kids, teens and grown-ups. With its extremely narrow turning radius, it is suitable for coasting slides, half-pipes, slalom runs, and roads. It is available in a free configuration of colors, lengths, skids or rollers. High-quality materials and a sturdy construction guarantee sledding fun for many generations. With its large range of rollers and skids, the racer can be used year-round. The "ScorpionRacer" can grow along with the user, as it can be expanded from three to four elements. Safety is ensured by providing reflectors and phosphorescent elements for nighttime fun.

RaceGear based in Eglisau, Switzerland develops high-quality sports equipment. The products are distinguished by their unique design, performance, modularity, multi-functionality and customization. The development of Toys and sportive leisure products constitute the company's key areas of operation.

PHOTOS: COURTESY OF THE DESIGNER

quadesign partner

The fully-automated coffee maker "Jura J7 / Nobel" has a thrilling perfected all-round design. Perfect coffee specialties, an exquisite look, and handling via a touch screen display appeal to gourmets and esthetes.
The sink "Franke PLANARIO" is in line with the requirements of modern esthetics with an unparalleled generously-proportioned base surface. It is the only sink that can accommodate entire pizza baking trays with standard dimensions.
"Swissray Radiography system ddRFormula" - featuring a tripod and a light panel, this digital system is very different from its predecessors. Most striking is the ambiance it adds to rooms in children's clinics where the brightly lit images distract the little ones from the treatment process.

As an experienced and competent partner for product development and design consulting, quadesign supports its customers from individual assignments to complex product systems. Its services increase the quality, image and added value of products and services to benefit producers and consumers. Numerous international design awards confirm the outstanding performance of the team and its commitment. Headquartered in Zug, quadesign operates in an orchestrated network with experts such as ergonomists, engineering specialists and manufacturers.

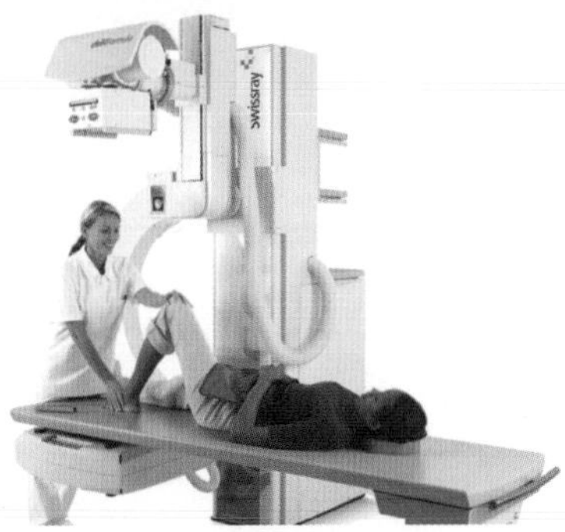

» Simple is difficult, difficult doesn't matter. «

PHOTOS: COURTESY OF QUODESIGN.

Christine Birkhoven

The limited series, “Stone age” and “Back” aim to take the preparation of foodstuffs to a sapient yet modern level. Material and craft meet each other, irreplaceable in their honesty and individuality. The objects are intuitive in their application, there are no directions for use, or wrong ways of using them. These kitchen utensils want to be handled: to feel the heavy, cold material and to recognise its handiness will turn the preparation of food into an irresistible pleasure.

POSTFOSSIL is a collective of emerging designers, which creates objects for the home, thinking about the post-fossil reality and putting their objects into the context of resource scarcity. The use of environmentally friendly and renewable resources is only the basis and POSTFOSSIL takes it to the next level. Fossil does not only stand for energy sources but also for social behaviour patterns. That’s where the initiators start.

» I consider Swiss design to be unpretentious and somehow reserved — otherwise conceptually very strong and intelligent. «

The fireplace set “Souffleur Ramón”, consists of a bellows and wood basket, which are both made of wood and leather. A bellows is not only a beautiful object with a very cozy character, but also reflects the energy required to start a fire. It is an invitation to take the time for lighting a really good fire, which will generate excellent glowing timbers.

“Pic” is made of stone and wood and does not need additional connections. Holes have been drilled into the edges at the underside of the table, in which the timber connectors of the table legs were anchored. The weight of the rock gives the table stability.

PHOTOS: FIREPLACE SET “SOUFFELUR RAMÓN”: MIRJAM GRAF; TABLE “PIC”: PHILIPP HAENGER; KITCHEN UTENSILS: “STONE TOOLS”: MATTHIAS JURT

Othmar Mühlebach Produktgestaltung

The Toaster "Printing Your Toast" promises fun toasting. Similar to a printer, up to six pieces of bread are placed in the feeder. At the push of a button they are individually moved past the heating element, fall into the bowl, and are ready for eating.
The navigation platform "Gina" is a mobile measuring and display device that supports the spatial orientation during operations. It was developed for the ARTORG Center for Biomedical Engineering, which researches computer and image based surgery technologies.
The sewing machine "Animo" is wonderfully suited for integration into the lifestyle of modern performers. It offers optimal ergonomics combined with sophisticated details.

Design must pay off - for the company, the user and the designer. Consciously designed product lines can give companies a distinguished character. This requires target-oriented esthetics, as well as functional, ergonomic, economic, and ecological aspects. Users want the design to appeal to their emotions to allow them to communicate their own lifestyle. The innovative power of the design can only take full effect if the designer is a team partner from the start.

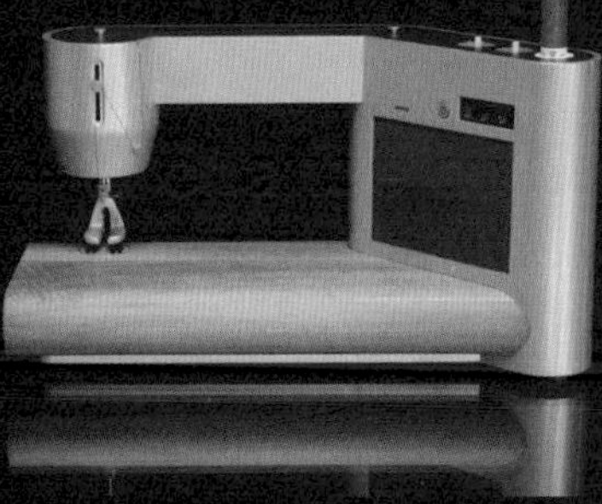

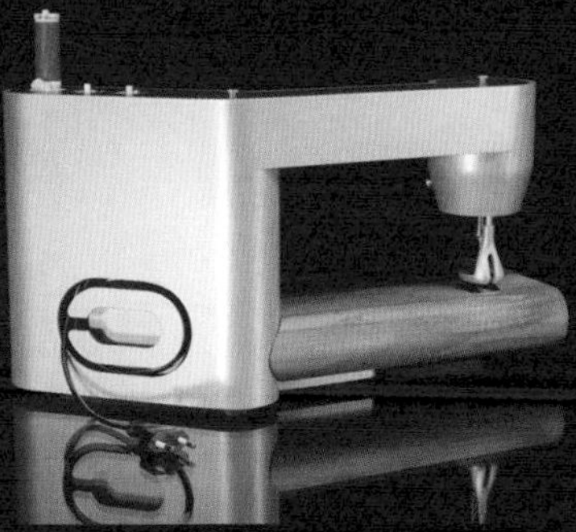

» A change of perspective leads to surprising possibilities ... «

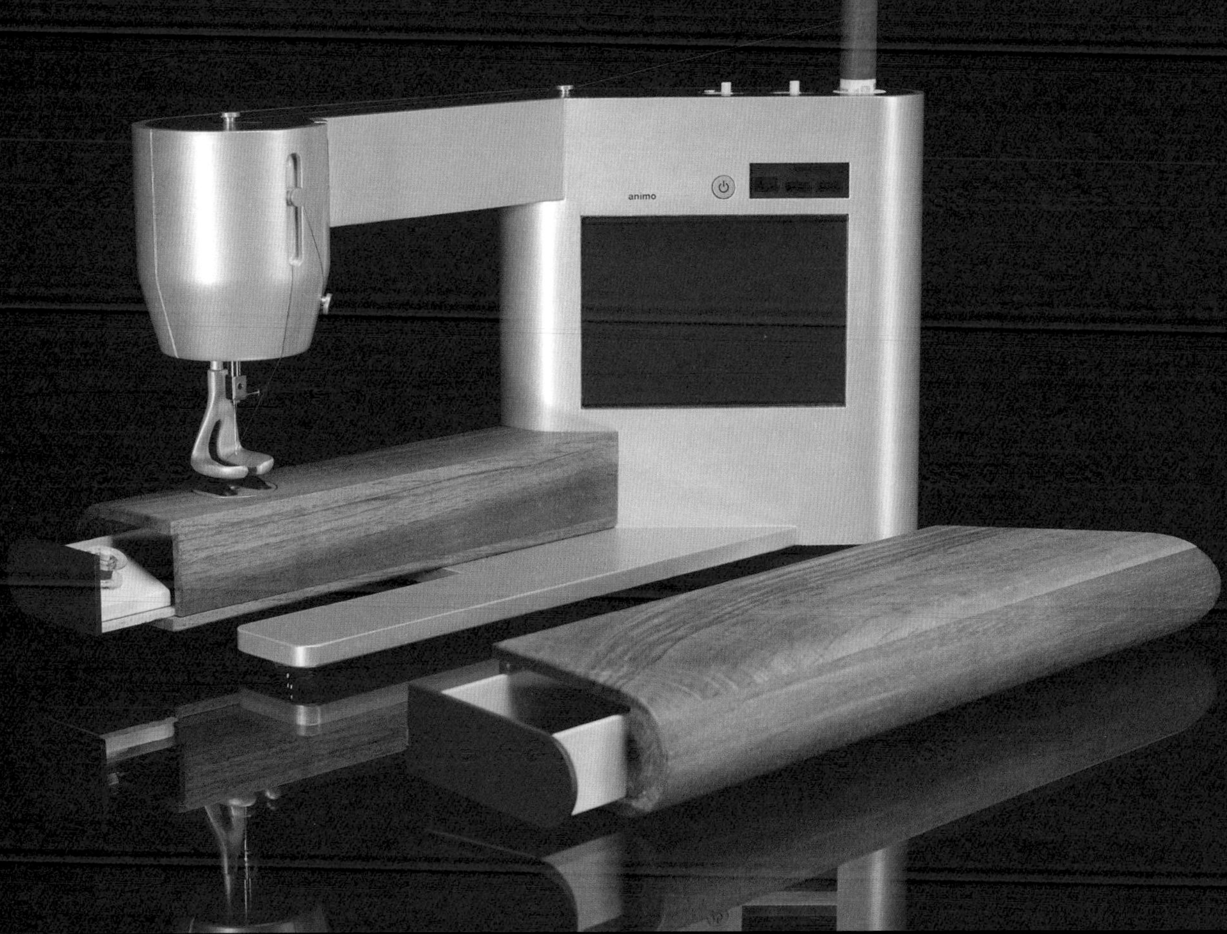

animo

PHOTOS: COURTESY OF THE DESIGNER

fuente Y fuente

In the works for Wenger, the approach was taken to re-strengthen the original design values by quoting the great classics and modernizing their most characteristic details. Furthermore, the goal was to find new ways of innovation other than just putting any blade in a sandwich between two covers.

Fuente Y fuente was founded in March 2006 by Designer Thilo Brunner - a.k.a. Thilo Fuente. From the very beginning, the goal of fuente Y fuente was to build up and preserve a portfolio with a vast variation of works. The range of projects extends from early street influenced work for Swatch (Instant Stores) to luxury projects like the jewelry for Audemars Piguet in 2009. According to Fuente, "Variation and being at home in several worlds is the biggest luxury one can get." Clients include typically Swiss companies like Swatch, Rado or Wenger.

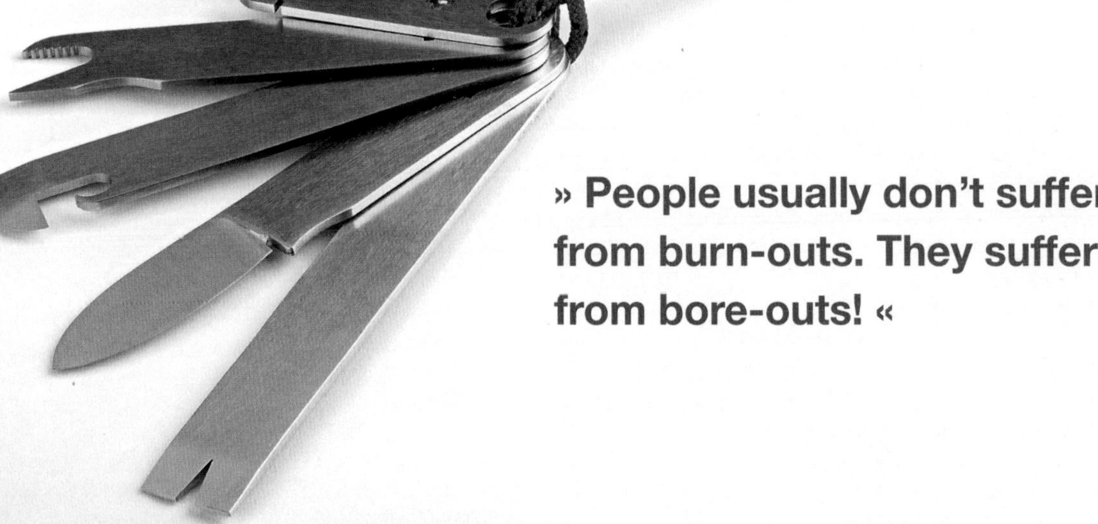

» People usually don't suffer from burn-outs. They suffer from bore-outs! «

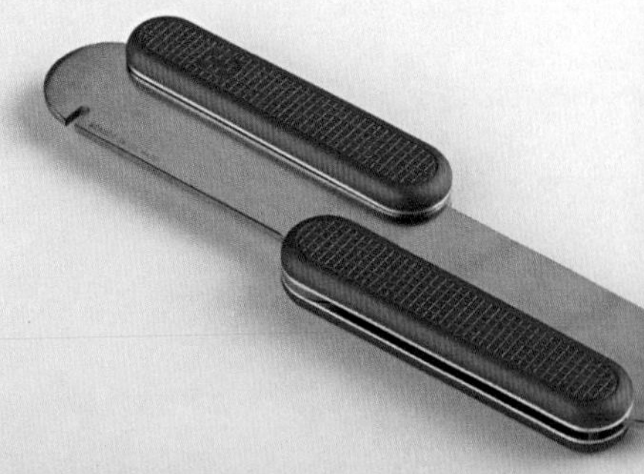

"ON Running" are simple yet highly functional running shoes. The Zurich based company ON was ready to take a new approach to performance footgear that can be summarized with the attributes: clear, reduced, adult.
For TAG Aviation, fuente y fuente developed a table object like a porcelain cloud penetrated by a golden air plane.

PHOTOS: WENGER MESSER: C2009 THILO FUENTE / ECAL. FOTOS: MICHEL BONVIN / ECAL
ON SCHUHE: C2009 THILO FUENTE FOTOS: SCHLEGEL I VONARBURG

Claudia Heiniger

"FAM_filzalmuro" is a wall hanging that generates psychological warmth in the room when covered by articles of clothing. This allows users to turn down the heating and subsequently save oil.

"Bivano-Seat For Two" is a seat with a space-saving design for small homes. During the cutting already, the frame reduces the amount of used materials. The cover made of elastic strips provides a comfortable seating area with minimized materials.

» Design explores and discovers, tries out, plays and gains experience. «

In 2007, young Swiss designers founded the POSTFOSSIL group with the aim of regularly exchanging ideas and concepts related to current and potential design-related issues. Since its initiation, the group has been dealing with issues relating to the future handling of resources and the associated ramifications for product design. Today, following several successful exhibitions, the group consists of six designers who jointly implement products and exhibitions, hold lectures, and organize workshops.

PHOTOS: COURTESY OF THE DESIGNER

Jura

"ENA-Series" by CANDIO & BÜTTLER is JURA's most successful product, received the red dot design award in 2008 as well as the Good Design Award. In 2010, the German lifestyle magazine "Schöner Wohnen" included it in its list of "New classics." These awards recognized the high design quality, simple handling and energy efficiency of the coffee makers. Bright colors such as Coffee Cherry Red or Coffee Leaf Green are coupled with an innovative shape. With a width of only 23.8 centimeters, the machines are slightly tilted towards the user. The latest addition to the series, the "ENA 9 One Touch", offers two separate spout systems for milk and coffee variations at the touch of a button without milk residues.

With the "IMPRESSA Z" coffee makers, the most individual preparations can be easily programmed at the touch of a button. For the first time, the "IMPRESSA 7" features a height-adjustable cappuccino spout for cappuccino and latte macchiato, accommodating cups up to 153 millimeter in height. Integrated cup illumination allows the coffee variations to appear amber-colored or white.

In 1931 Leo Henzirohs established JURA Elektroapparate AG in Niederbuchsiten. The community is located near the southern foot of the Jura mountain range, from which the company derived its name. Today, the company is still based at the same location, selling household and electronic appliances. In Switzerland especially, JURA was renowned for its household appliances, most notably pressing irons. Starting in the 1980s, the JURA brand focused on espresso and coffee makers. Today, it is the global market leader in this sector.

» Swiss design turns coffee makers into interior design elements. «

HOTOS: JONAS SPENGLER FOR JURA

Andreas Kreienbühl was Art Director at BBDO in Zurich, ZOF Inc. Visual Communications in New York, and at Agentur für Innovation, Public Relations und Werbung (IPW AG) in Basel. In 2000 he co-founded the communications and design agency 9•6, headquartered in Basel.
9•6, Conceptional Worlds | St. Johanns-Vorstadt 17 | 4056 Basel
T +41.61.2619610 | F +41.61.2619611 | tete-a-tete@9--6.com | www.9--6.com

---

Marcus Gossolt, born 1969, is an architect, artist and advertiser. Together with Johannes M. Hedinger, he established the art label Com&Com in 1997. Marcus Gossolt studied architecture and art at the Höhere Schule für Gestaltung in Basel. In 2005 he established the Alltag agency together with Philipp Lämmlin.

Philipp Lämmlin, born 1969, studied marketing at the University of St.Gallen (HSG). During his senior year, he established the Internet agency namics ag together with two colleagues. In 2005 he established the Alltag agency together with Marcus Gossolt.
Alltag Agentur GmbH | Teufenerstrasse 95 | 9000 St. Gallen
T +41.71.5343855 | info@alltagagentur.ch | www.alltagagentur.ch

---

Philippe Vogt studied photography, philosophy and mechanics and has worked as a photographer, gallery owner and exhibition organizer. Since 1984 he has been working fulltime as a product designer. His motto is: new ways lead to new realities with wit and surprising solutions.
ARCA-SWISS Internatonal | 29 quartier de l'europe | 25048 Besancon, France
T +33.381.854060 | F +33.381.854069 | arca-swiss@wanadoo.fr

Stéphanie Bächler graduated as a fabric designer from HSLU Lucerne. After graduation, she mainly works for Jakob Schläpfer in St. Gallen where she develops creative fabrics and products for office settings.
stéphanie bächler | Rosenbergstrasse 42 a | 9000 St. Gallen
T +41.79.5624670 | info@stephaniebaechler.com | www.stephaniebaechler.com

---

Inés Bader graduated in 1984 from the Schule für Gestaltung in Basel. Since 1991 she has been creating socks and neck scarves. From 1992 to 2001 she was a visiting lecturer for knitted fabrics at the Hochschule für Gestaltung in Basel. Since 1996 she has been dedicating herself to her collections.
Inés Bader Textildesign | Sevogelstrasse 55 | 4052 Basel
T +41.61.2717684 | ines.bader@bluewin.ch | www.inesbader.ch

Rolf Senti, former professional bicyclist and owner of Bagno Sasso AG has been in charge of the company since 1985. Senti is passionate about expressive and noble design. In cooperation with international architects, designers and artists, he creates individual stylish bathrooms.
Bagno Sasso AG | Schulstrasse 76 | 7302 Landquart
T +41.81.3223868 | F +41.81.3223081 | info@bagnosasso.ch | www.bagnosasso.ch

---

Karin Maurer (*1970), Manuela Helg (*1967). The designers studied textile design from 1992 to 1996 at the Hochschule für Gestaltung und Kunst in Zurich. In the year of their graduation they founded the label Beige. Since then they have been developing their own collections and participated very successfully in exhibitions.
Beige | Josefstrasse 10 | 8005 Zurich
T +41.44.2727422 | F +41.44.2727422 | mail@beige.ch | www.beige.ch

---

After receiving vocational training as a constructional engineering draftsman from 1999 to 2003 at Müller + Messerli AG in Thun, David Bernet worked at the architecture firm of Gerber Schüpbach. In 2005 he received a diploma in design from GIB Bern. Since 2007 he has been working part time at Tecasia AG.
David Bernet | info@d-ber.net | www.d-ber.net

Christine Birkhoven (*1979) born and raised in Santiago de Chile, completed several training courses at design studios in Spain, Germany and Switzerland while working on her degree in industrial design. After receiving her diploma in the year 2004, she has been working as an independent designer with a focus on furniture, accessories, and sustainability.
POSTFOSSIL | Neugasse 59 | 8005 Zurich
christine@postfossil.ch | www.postfossil.ch

Thomas Blank has been working with glass for thirteen years. After graduating with a degree in fine arts from San Francisco State University he decided to return to Switzerland. Since the year 2001 he has been working as an independent glassmaker in Bern.
studio thomas blank | Veilchenweg 6 | 3018 Bern
T +41.0.78.7101410 | info@studio.ch | www.studio.ch

Anna Blattert is an industrial designer and structural engineering draftswoman. Since the year 2006 she has been working as a self-employed designer and research assistant at HS Luzern, department of product design. Since the year 2009, she has been a visiting lecturer for industrial design at the FHNW.
Postfossil | Neugasse 59 | 8005 Zurich
info@postfossil.ch | www.postfossil.ch

Jean-Philippe Bonzon, Swiss and Argentinean, lives and works between Shanghai, China and Lausanne, Switzerland, where he obtained his degree in Industrial Design and Products at ECAL. During the past years, he has exhibited his various works in New York, Cologne, and Lausanne.
Jean-Philippe Bonzon Designer | Route du Villars 41 | 1024 Écublens
T +41.21.6915989 | F +41.21.96915969 | info@jpbd.ch | www.jpbd.ch

Alain Jost (*1975) visited the Swiss Federal Polytechnical School Lausanne - Architecture. He received his diploma in product design in 2000 from the Swiss School for Fine Arts and Design Basel. In 2000, he founded the label brandnewdesign in Basel, where he works as independent designer.
brandnewdesign.ch | Basel
T +41.44.5865336 | info@brandnewdesign.ch | www.brandnewdesign.ch

Esther Brinkmann was born in 1953 in Baden (CH). She received her diploma as a jeweler from the School for Applied Arts, Geneva in 1978. She has extensive international teaching and lecturing experience and works and lives at the moment in Guangzhou, China.
Esther Brinkmann Bijoux | T +86.20.89269300 | F +86.20.38330453
esther.brinkmann@vtxmail.ch | www.estherbrinkmann.com

Isabel Bürgin has been working as a freelance fabric designer since 1986, creating her own carpet collections. In 1992, she received the Bayerischer Staatspreis (Bavarian national award) and was nominated in 2003 for the Swiss Design Award. From 2006 to 2009 she had a professorship for the design of textile products at the Kunsthochschule Kassel.
Isabel Bürgin Textilgestalterin | Klybeckstrasse 14 | 4057 Basel
T +41.61.6835636 | F +41.61.6835637 | mail@isabel-buergin.ch | www.isabel-buergin.ch

“Büro Destruct” is comprised of “MB” (Marc Brunner, *1970), “H1” (Heinz Reber, *1971), “HeiWid” (Heinz Widmer, *1967) and “Lopetz” (Lorenz Gianfreda, *1971). Co-founder “HGB Fideljus” (*1971) has been running the “Büro Discount” gallery and shop in Zurich since 2002.
Büro Destruct | Wasserwerkgasse 7 | 3011 Bern
T +41.31.3126383 | bd@burodestruct.net | www.burodestruct.net

Remo Caminada (*1974) enrolled in 2001 at the Hochschule für Gestaltung und Kunst in Zurich. In 2002 he switched to visual design and graduated in 2006. After working for Sean Perkins, North Design, and James Goggin, Practise, he established his own office.
Caminada | M +31.631.054122 | info@remocaminada.com | www.remocaminada.com

After receiving his diploma in industrial design from the Hochschule der Künste, Zurich, Ronald Büttler (*1968) worked for various design studios on projects in the areas of investment and consumer goods. In 2004, in cooperation with Manuel Candido he established the studio CANDIO & BÜTTLER, where he is in charge of industrial design.

After receiving a diploma in architecture from ETH Zurich and attending the Kunstakademie Düsseldorf as a visiting student, Manuel Candio (*1967) worked for several years in Berlin. In 2004, in cooperation with Ronald Büttler, he established the studio CANDIO & BÜTTLER, where he is in charge of architecture and interior finishing.
CANDIO & BÜTTLER | Zwinglistrasse 34a | 8004 Zurich | T +41.44.2719290
F +41.44.2719158 | info@candiobuettler.ch | www.candiobuettler.ch

Carolina Cerbaro (*1976) received her diploma as a visual designer from the Hochschule für Gestaltung und Kunst, Zurich. After graduation, she has been working independently on contract design projects, group projects and exhibitions.
CC | Carolina Cerbaro | Basel | T +41.44.5081098 | matuschkarossija@no-log.org

Matthias Etter (*1954) was trained as a mechanical engineer and a social education worker. He worked with disabled individuals and as a teacher of metal working. Since 1999 he has been working in the management, promotion, presentation and development of games and concepts for cuboro AG.
cuboro AG | 6086 Hasliberg Reuti
T +41.33.9715950 | F +41.33.9715951 | info@cuboro.ch | www.cuboro.ch

Martino d'Esposito (*1976) is an industrial designer living and working in Lausanne. He attended the Fine Arts School of Vevey and received his Master's of Arts in the year 2004 from ECAL. Today he works as an independent product designer and lecturer at ECAL.

Alexandre Gaillard (*1976) graduated with a degree in high-precision mechanics in 1998. He later received a bachelor's degree in product design from ECAL. Today he works together with Martino d'Esposito as a product designer in his own company and teaches technical drawing at ECAL.
d'Esposito & Gailla | Chemin du Boisy 47 | 1004 Lausanne | d'Esposito
T +41.76.3476686 | Gaillard T +41.79.7508279 | www.despositogaillard.com

Florin Baeriswyl graduated in 1987 from the Hochschule für Kunst und Gestaltung, Zurich with a degree in industrial design. In his view, design is an integral part of the client's communication strategy through which the identity of a company is reflected in its products.
dai design | Grubenstrasse 45 | 8045 Zurich
T +41.44.4562600 | F +41.44.4562616 | contact@dai.ch | www.dai.ch

Eva Katharina Bruggmann was trained as a professional goldsmith. This was followed by training as a gemologist in Idar-Oberstein, a guest study program at the Zeichenakademie Hanau, and a degree in jewelry and product design from HGK Zurich. Since 1994 she has been operating her own studio in Zurich.
daughter of eve, eva katharina bruggmann | Postfach 5256 | 8050 Zurich
T +41.44.8109404 | F +41.44.8109405 | info@daughterofeve.ch | www.daughterofeve.ch

Frédéric Dedelley, born 1964, studied Industrial Design at the ECAL, Lausanne and at Art Center College of Design (Europe), La Tour-de-Peilz. In 1995, he established a design studio in Zurich, where he conceives products, furniture, exhibitions and interiors.
Frédéric Dedelley | Gerechtigkeitsgasse 2 | 8001 Zurich
T +41.44.2404828 | fd@fredericdedelley.ch | www.fredericdedelley.ch

Fabian Stacoff first completed his vocational training as a sales clerk before being trained as a decoration designer at Idee AG Zurich. Before establishing his own company Dessert in 2003 as an independent graphic designer, he worked in project development for Winkler Gestaltung in Zurich.

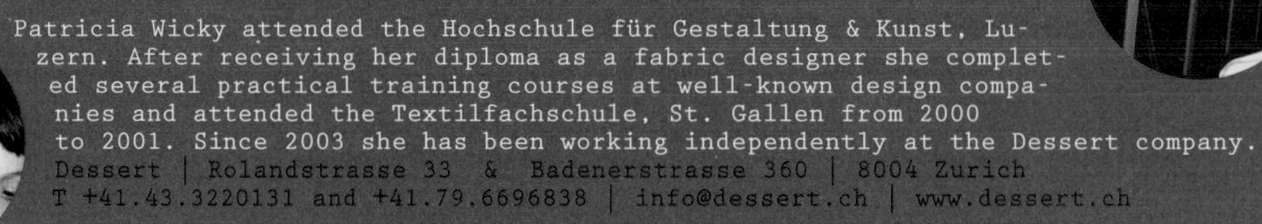

Patricia Wicky attended the Hochschule für Gestaltung & Kunst, Luzern. After receiving her diploma as a fabric designer she completed several practical training courses at well-known design companies and attended the Textilfachschule, St. Gallen from 2000 to 2001. Since 2003 she has been working independently at the Dessert company.
Dessert | Rolandstrasse 33 & Badenerstrasse 360 | 8004 Zurich
T +41.43.3220131 and +41.79.6696838 | info@dessert.ch | www.dessert.ch

Catherine Dubler (*1981) was trained as a seamstress. She worked for shoe designer Anita Moser, before pursuing a master's degree from 2007 to 2009 at the London College of Fashion, University of the Arts. Today she works as a fashion designer.
Catherine Dubler | Gilgenbergerstrasse 21 | 4053 Basel
T +41.61.5564126 | M +41.61.5564126 | 2catherine.dubler@gmail.com | www.nulz.ch

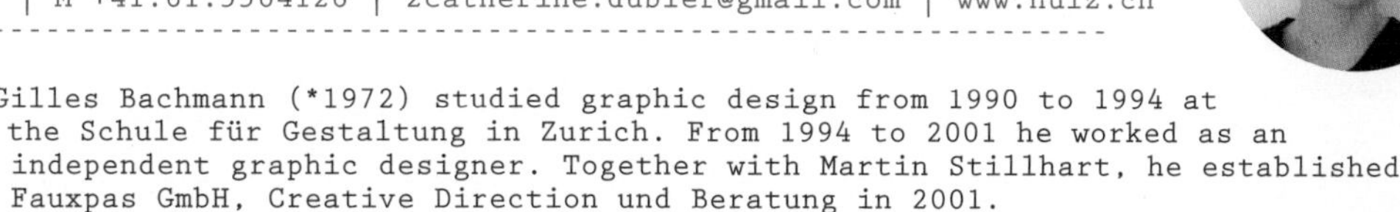

Gilles Bachmann (*1972) studied graphic design from 1990 to 1994 at the Schule für Gestaltung in Zurich. From 1994 to 2001 he worked as an independent graphic designer. Together with Martin Stillhart, he established Fauxpas GmbH, Creative Direction und Beratung in 2001.

After completing his professional training as a typographer from 1986-1990, Martin Stillhart (*1969) enhanced his expertise by studying typographic design at the Schule für Gestaltung in Basel. From 1994 to 2001 he worked as an independent graphic designer. Together with Gilles Bachmann, he established Fauxpas GmbH, Creative Direction und Beratung in 2001.
Fauxpas GmbH | Zweierstrasse 129 | 8003 Zurich
T +41.43.3331105 | F +41.43.3331175 | contact@fauxpas.ch | www.fauxpas.ch

After completing her training as a structural engineering draughtswoman, Caroline Flueler (*1968 in Zug) completed a five year degree program in fabric design. After graduation, she founded the label «Caroline Flueler, Switzerland», where she specialized in the design of accessories and cover fabrics in her unique style.
Caroline Flueler, Switzerland | Räbmatt 6 | 6317 Oberwil-Zug
T +41.41.7121349 | cf@caroline-flueler.com | www.caroline-flueler.com

Bettina Geistlich (*1972) completed her vocational training as a goldsmith and collected practical experience at the goldsmiths Kurt Neukomm and Rolf Müller. From 2001 to 2005 she studied at the specialized department of precious stones and jewelry design of the Fachhochschule Trier in Idar-Oberstein. She established her own workshop in Lucerne in the year 2007.
formabina schmuckgestaltung | Reussinsel 46 | 6003 Luzern
T +41.41.2406080 | F +41.41.2406081 | info@formabina.ch | www.formabina.ch

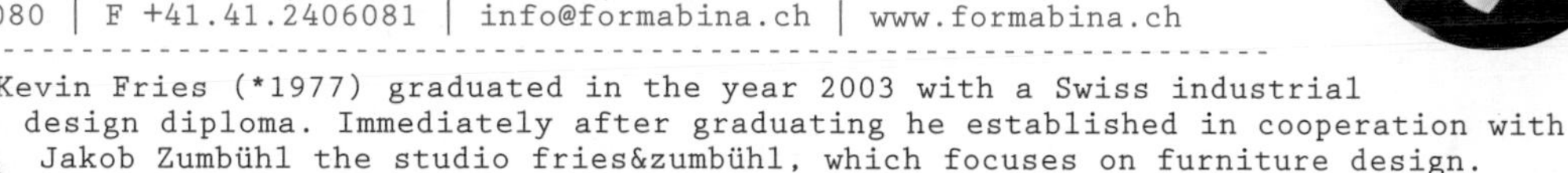

Kevin Fries (*1977) graduated in the year 2003 with a Swiss industrial design diploma. Immediately after graduating he established in cooperation with Jakob Zumbühl the studio fries&zumbühl, which focuses on furniture design.

Jakob Zumbühl (*1978) graduated in the year 2003 with a Swiss industrial design diploma. Immediately after graduating he established in cooperation with Kevin Fries the studio fries&zumbühl, which focuses on furniture design and has already received many awards.
fries&zumbühl | Lessingstrasse 13 | 8002 Zurich
T +41.43.3335330 | F +41.43.3449558 | mail@frieszumbuehl.ch | www.frieszumbuehl.ch

Thilo Fuente (*1977) worked from 1998-2001 in the product management of Swatch. In 2002 he enrolled in industrial design at FHNW and graduated in 2006. Afterwards he founded fuente Y fuente. In 2008 he took up, parallel to his work, postgraduate studies at ECAL, which he completed in 2009.
fuente Y fuente | Atelier 2 / Neugasse 151 | 8005 Zurich
T +41.43.5414894 | fullcontact@fuenteyfuente.ch | www.fuenteyfuente.ch

Yves Béhar, born 1967 in Lausanne, is one of the world's leading industrial designers. He first studied industrial design at the Swiss branch of the «Art Center College of Design» in La Tour-de-Peilz, then enrolled at the main college in Pasadena, California, where he graduated with a BSc in Industrial Design. He then worked for the companies Frogdesign and Lunar Design. He is dean of the industrial design department at the California College of the Arts. In 1999 he established Fuseproject in San Francisco.
fuseproject | 528 Folsom Street | San Francisco, CA 94105, USA
T +1.415.9081492 | F +1.415.9081491 | info@fuseproject.com | www.fuseproject.com

Daniel Gafner (*1977) lives and works in Zurich. He received a diploma as cabinet maker in 1998 and as industrial designer in 2006. Since 2008 he has been working as an independent designer in the fields of interior design, product design, fashion and art. In 2009 he led the "critical design" workshop as a lecturer at the FHNW.

Daniel Gafner | Hermetschloostrasse 70 | 8048 Zurich
T +41.78.8595627 | info@danielgafner.ch | www.danielgafner.ch

Elif Gedik was trained as a seamstress in Bern, followed by training as a textile trader in Zurich. She then pursued professional training as a stylist in London. After its completion she has been working independently in this area. She has a studio in Aarberg and in Paris.

Elif Gedik | Sägeweg 17 | 3270 Aarberg
T + 41.79.7046514 | info@elifgedik.ch | www.elifgedik.ch

Alexis Georgacopoulos (*1976) lives and works in Lausanne. His works are associated with the ECAL-University of Art and Design Lausanne, where he was the head of the industrial design department from 2000 to 2008. In parallel, he has been developing his own practice working in products, furniture and exhibition design.

Alexis Georgacopoulos Industrial Design | 3, Place Chauderon | 1006 Lausanne
T +41.21.3120110 | info@georgacopoulos.com | www.georgacopoulos.com

Philipp Gilgen, born 1976, was trained from 1993 to 1997 as an industrial design draftsman. From 2004 to 2008 he studied Industrial Design at the Fachhochschule Nordwestschweiz. Since 2008 he has been working as an industrial designer for customers in the consumer product, public transportation, as well as furniture and lamp design sectors.

Philipp Gilgen Industrial Designer | Reichensteinerstrasse 7 | 4053 Basel
T +41.79.2090074 | hello@philippgilgen.ch | www.philippgilgen.ch

Carmen Greutmann is an industrial engineering draftswoman by profession. In the year 1984 she established together with Urs Greutmann the Greutmann Bolzern Design studio in Zurich. She studied at the Hochschule für Gestaltung und Kunst in Zurich from where she received a diploma as an interior designer.

Urs Greutmann established in 1984 together with Carmen Greutmann the Greutmann Bolzern design studio in Zurich. He is an industrial engineering draftsman by profession and studied from 1980 und 1984 at Hochschule für Gestaltung und Kunst in Zurich, from which he received a diploma as an industrial designer.

greutmann bolzern designstudio | Sihlquai 268 | 8005 Zurich
T +41.44.4405588 | F +41.44.4405580 | carmen.greutmann@gbdesign.ch
urs.greutmann@gbdesign.ch | www.gbdesign.ch

Claudia Vera Güdel, *1972 in Zurich, Switzerland, lives in Basel. She studied fashion design at HGK Basel, Körper & Kleid (body and clothing) department. She gained practical work experience while working with the fashion designer Eduardo Lucero in LA, with fashion designer Anna Sui N.Y., and at the Metropolitan Opera in New York.

Claudia Güdel | Markgräflerstrasse 34 | 4057 Basel | T +41.61.6311102
F +41.61.3811976 | claudia@claudiagudel.ch | www.claudiagudel.ch

Simone Gugger (*1974) completed her vocational training as a decorator in 1994. In 1997 she enrolled at the Hochschule für Gestaltung in Zurich at the department of jewelry and tools. Before graduating in the year 2001 she already established her studio in Zurich.

Simone Gugger | Hardstrasse 219/K1 | 8005 Zurich
T +41.43.3669059 | schmuck@simonegugger.ch | www.simonegugger.ch

Alfredo Häberli was born in 1964 in Buenos Aires, Argentina. Today he is an internationally established designer with headquarters in Zurich. His designs combine tradition and innovation as well as wit and curiosity. This results in products with powerful emotions and a great deal of functionality, which he conceives for famous companies in the design sector.

Alfredo Häberli Design Development | Seefeldstrasse 301a | 8008 Zurich
T +41.44.3803230 | F +41.44.3803239
studio@alfredo-haeberli.com | www.alfredo-haeberli.com

Florian Hauswirth studied industrial design at the FHNW, after completing his vocational training with a diploma in technical model construction. He gained initial work experience at Vogt+Weizenegger in Berlin and at BarberOsgerby in London. He has been working as an independent designer since 2006.
Florian Hauswirth | Libellenweg 1 | 2502 Biel
T +41.79.4171054 | florian@postfossil.ch | www.florianhauswirth.ch

Claudia Heiniger graduated as an elementary and junior high teacher in the year 1995. In 2006 she received her diploma in industrial design and subsequently joined GANSAM Partners Seoul. Since 2008 she has been working independently in Switzerland and Italy. In the same year, she became a member of POST-FOSSIL.
Claudia Heiniger c/o Postfossil | Neugasse 59 | 8005 Zurich
T +39.3319473762 | info@postfossil.ch | www.postfossil.ch

After graduating from high school, Heiko Hillig (*1971) attended the Hochschule für Kunst und Design Burg Giebichenstein in Halle/Saale. After receiving his diploma, he worked as a product designer for Erzi. Since 1997 he has repeatedly created toys for Naef Spiele AG as well as independent artistic works based on paper.
Heiko Hillig | Grendelweg 5 | 4314 Zeiningen
T +41.79.2977100 | hillig@bluewin.ch

Alex Hochstrasser (*1973) attended the Industrial Design program of the School of Art and Design in Zurich. After different internships at IDEO San Francisco, IDEO Tokyo, and Smart Design New York among others, he received his diploma as an Industrial Designer HFG in 2000. Since 2002 he has been working for ACTIVE PEOPLE.
Alex Hochstrasser Industrial Design | Seefeldstrasse 178 | 8008 Zurich
T +41.43.4886282 | F +41.43.4886281
mail@alex-hochstrasser.ch | www.alex-hochstrasser.ch

Vinzenz Blaas (corporate design, graduate designer) already worked for Lowe AG, Neutral AG, Department, Jung von Matt AG, Publicis AG, Voser Werbung AG and others. He received his diploma as a visual designer from the Hochschule für Gestaltung und Kunst in Zurich.

Philipp Schubiger (strategy, business communication, graduate designer) already worked as an art director at Netvertising, Grey, Musqueteers. He received his diploma in visual design from the Hochschule für Gestaltung und Kunst in Zurich.

Jonas Voegeli (Editorial, Books, Gestalter FH) founded and co-founded JTV and The Remingtons. He graduated from Hochschule für Gestaltung und Kunst in Zurich and already worked as a co-art director for Das Magazin, Musqueteers, Neutral, Müller+Hess, AxisDesign, Graphics International, and E-Fact.
Hubertus Design | Letzigraben 114 | 8047 Zurich
T +41.43.9600233 | info@hubertus-design.ch | www.hubertus-design.ch

In his youth, Heinz Julen (*1964) already reconstructed many old houses in the Wallis canton together with his father. In 1980 he established the first mountain studio in Findeln, and in 1984 he opened the Heinz Julen gallery in the basement of an apparel store in Zermatt. Following numerous projects in the area of creative arts, architecture and design, he established the architecture firm Heinz Julen Idee in 2008.
Heinz Julen | Hofmattstrasse 4 | 3920 Zermatt
T +41.27.9677177 | F +41.27.9677175 | www.heinzjulen.com

Michèle Kägi is a designer with international experience and extensive professional training. She worked for the trendy company Jet Set Sportswear St. Moritz, Erica Matile Zurich and as senior designer for the haute couture label Louis Féraud in Germany and Paris, where she was also in charge of the prêt-à-porter line. Since 2003 she has been developing various skirt collections in her own studio in Zurich. In 2009, she established her own store.
roecke.ch - Michèle Kägi | Am Wasser 127 | 8049 Zurich
M +41.79.5498524 | michelekaegi@roecke.ch | www.roecke.ch

Susan D. Korb (*1963) studied architecture from 1986 to 1992 at Universität Stuttgart. In 1989 she already established KORB + KORB together with Daniel Korb. The company focuses on comprehensive design including interior refurnishing and lighting. In 1996, they founded the KORB + KORB subsidiary in Baden/Switzerland, which was expanded in 1999 to include marketing and communication services.

Daniel Korb (*1953) holds a degree in interior design. He studied interior design at the Fachhochschule für Technik in Stuttgart. In 1990 his first product, "CONNECT" was introduced at the Orgatec trade fair. His products have received a wide variety of international design awards.

KORB + KORB | Schartenstrasse 3 | 5400 Baden
T +41.56.2001420 | F +41.56.2001424 | info@korb-korb.ch | www.korb-korb.ch

Florian Kräutli is originally from Winterthur. After completing the prep course at the Hochschule für Gestaltung und Kunst in Lucerne, he moved to the Netherlands and enrolled at the Design Academy Eindhoven. After graduation he remained in Eindhoven, where he is self-employed and works in collaboration with Kathy Ludwig.

Florian Kräutli | 1e Akkermuntstraat 16 | 5643DK Eindhoven
T +31.6.21258998 | florian@kraeutli.com | www.kraeutli.com

Lovis Caputo lives and works in Zurich. She received her diploma in product design from the Hochschule für Gestaltung in Zurich. Since 2006, she has been working with Sarah Kueng under the label Kueng Caputo on the development of everyday objects with an ironic and playful touch.

Sarah Kueng lives and works in Zurich. She received her diploma in product design from the Hochschule für Gestaltung in Zurich. Since 2006, she has been working with Lovis Caputo under the label Kueng Caputo on the development of everyday objects with an ironic and playful touch.

Kueng Caputo | Leimbachstrasse 5 | 8041 Zurich
T +41.76.4115794 | contact@kueng-caputo.ch | www.kueng-caputo.ch

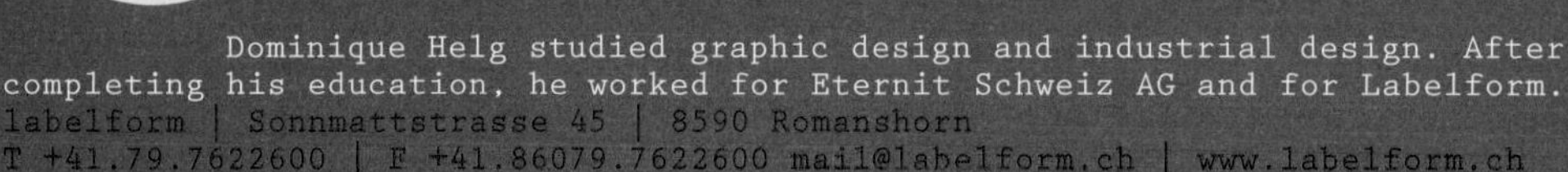

Dominique Helg studied graphic design and industrial design. After completing his education, he worked for Eternit Schweiz AG and for Labelform.

labelform | Sonnmattstrasse 45 | 8590 Romanshorn
T +41.79.7622600 | F +41.86079.7622600 mail@labelform.ch | www.labelform.ch

Nicolas Le Moigne (*1979) received his bachelor's degree in product design in 2005 and his Master's in the same field in 2007. Before graduation, he worked as a teaching assistant at ECAL. After receiving his Master's, he worked as professor for the design department at ECAL and for the polytechnic school of Lausanne.

Nicolas Le Moigne | 17, avenue de Jurigoz | 1006 Lausanne
T +41.79.2044432 | nicolas_lm@hotmail.com | www.nicolaslemoigne.com

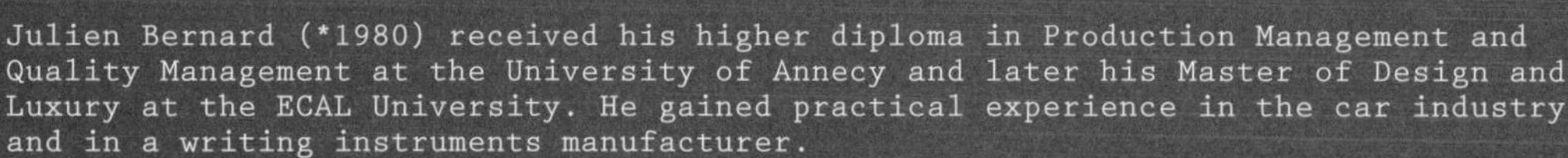

Julien Bernard (*1980) received his higher diploma in Production Management and Quality Management at the University of Annecy and later his Master of Design and Luxury at the ECAL University. He gained practical experience in the car industry and in a writing instruments manufacturer.

Luc Swen | rue de Lausanne 45-47 | 1201 Genève
T +33.6.84215703 | lucswen@gmail.com | www.lucswen.com

Natalie Luder was born in 1973 in Rüti ZH, Switzerland. From 1999 to 2003 she attended the Haute Ecole des Arts Appliqués, department of Bijou/Objet in Geneva, and from 2001 to 2002 the Gerrit Rietveld Academie Amsterdam, Department Edelsmeden. Since 2004 she has been working at her own studio in Zurich.

Natalie Luder | Hermetschloostrasse 70 | 8048 Zurich | T +41.77.4106115
info@natalieluder.ch | www.natalieluder.ch

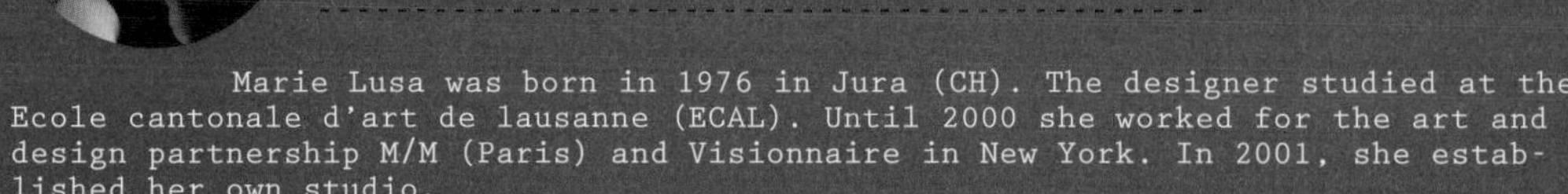

Marie Lusa was born in 1976 in Jura (CH). The designer studied at the Ecole cantonale d'art de lausanne (ECAL). Until 2000 she worked for the art and design partnership M/M (Paris) and Visionnaire in New York. In 2001, she established her own studio.

Marie Lusa | Gamperstrasse 8 | 8004 Zurich | T +41.78.6737078
lusa@derrierelacolline.net | www.marielusa.net

Christophe Marchand (*1965) was trained as a cabinet maker at the Schule für Gestaltung, Zurich. He then attended the Höhere Schule für Gestaltung in Zurich. Today he works as a designer, managing director and professor, as well as being a member of various design boards.
Christophe Marchand Design | Untere Heslibachstrasse 39 | 8700 Küsnacht
T +41.44.3802848 | F +41.44.3802847
chm@christophemarchand.ch | www.christophemarchand.ch

David, born 1985 in Lausanne, Switzerland commutes between Lausanne and New York. His areas of specialization are design and typographic compositions.

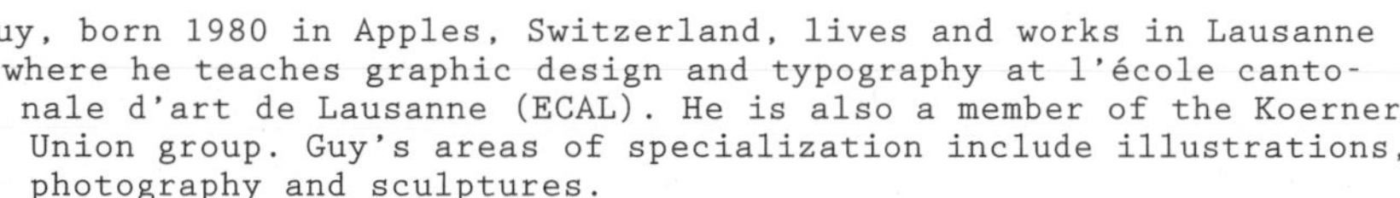

Guy, born 1980 in Apples, Switzerland, lives and works in Lausanne where he teaches graphic design and typography at l'école cantonale d'art de Lausanne (ECAL). He is also a member of the Koerner Union group. Guy's areas of specialization include illustrations, photography and sculptures.

Jean, born 1983 in Perpignan, France, is a photographer and graphic designer. Since 2008 he has been living and working in Lausanne, Switzerland, where he joined the Maximage group. Jean launched his career in Paris in 2003, then moved to Brussels. Jean's areas of specialization include photo editing, production and management.
Maximage Group | Pontaise 15 | 1018 Lausanne
T +41.78.8840414 | maxi@maximage.biz | www.maximage.biz

Wolfgang K. Meyer-Hayoz (*1947) studied mechanical engineering, visual communications and industrial design and graduated from the Staatliche Akademie der bildenden Künste in Stuttgart. In 1985 he founded Meyer-Hayoz Design Engineering AG in Switzerland.
Meyer-Hayoz Design Engineering AG | Jägerstrasse 2 | 8406 Winterthur
T +41.52.2090101 | F +41.52.2090109
info.ch@meyer-hayoz.com | www.meyer-hayoz.com

Christa Michel lives and works in Zurich and Lucerne. After her graduation as a fabric designer from the Hochschule für Gestaltung in Zurich, she launched her career as a knitwear designer at her own studio. From 2003 to 2010 she also worked as a lecturer for knit design at HSLU in Lucerne.
Christa Michel Knitwear | T +41.44.2420592 | F +41.44.2420592
info@christamichel.com | www.christamichel.com

Therese Naef is the CEO/partner of milani design & consulting AG. She completed her vocational training in architectural model making before graduating with a degree in industrial design from the Hochschule für Gestaltung und Kunst in Zurich. In addition to her work at milani design & consulting AG she also works as a private lecturer on product design.

Britta Pukall is the owner/managing partner of milani design & consulting AG. She studied design at the universities of Kassel and Vienna and graduated with a Magister degree. She worked for Frog Design and Schott Glaswerke before joining milani design & consulting AG.
milani design & consulting AG | Seestrasse 95 | 8800 Thalwil
T +41.44.9147474 | F +41.44.9147475 | hello@milani.ch | www.milani.ch

----

Anita Moser works in Basel, where she has been designing timeless collections of women's and men's shoes since 2003. During the prototype phase, the designer transfers her work venue to the production company to support the creation of the models on location. Her models combine exciting designs with practicality.
Anita Moser | Elsässerstrasse 248 | 4056 Basel
T +41.76.335 0168 | info@anitamoser.ch | www.anitamoser.ch

Butch Gaudy (*1959), lives and works in Bern, Grindelwald, and San Francisco. In 1981 the bike pioneer introduced the Mountain bike to Switzerland and founded the brand MTB CYCLETECH. Butch became famous in 1989 with his "SIMPLICITY," a radically reduced "2-speed bike with a coaster brake."
MTB Cycletech - Velobaze AG | Wagistrasse 7 | 8952 Schlieren
T +41.44.7732020 | F +41.44.7732022 | hello@velo.com | www.mtbcycletech.com

----

After gaining practical experience as a technical model constructor and graduating with a degree in interior design, Othmar Muehlebach worked for different furniture manufacturers in the metal and system furniture sector. In 2006 he studied industrial design at the FHNW in Aarau. In addition to his work as a designer, he is writing his master's thesis on the topic of corporate product design.
Mühlebach Produktgestaltung | Flüelistrasse 35a | 6064 Kerns
T +41.41.6220760 | F +41.41.6220761
othmar@produktgestaltung.ch | www.produktgestaltung.ch

Vito Noto (*1955) grew up in Switzerland and Italy where he studied at the Politecnico di Design in Milan. He gained professional experience in various renowned European design companies. He established the design studio Vito Noto in 1982.
Vito Noto Product Design | Via dei Circoli | 6965 Cadro | T +41.91.9434561
F +41.91.9434521 | office@vitonotodesign.com | www.vitonotodesign.com

After completing his vocational training as an interior decorator, Jürg Amman (*1969) gained first work experience in Basel, Lausanne und Zurich. In 1998 he graduated with a degree in interior and product design from HSfG Basel and Cooper Union School of Arts and Architecture in New York.
PIURIC | Walchestrasse 34 | 8006 Zurich | T +41.44.3624200 | F +41.44.3624209
mail@piuric.ch | www.piuric.ch

Annina Gähwiler graduated in 2006 with a degree in industrial design from FHNW, Gestaltung und Kunst, Aarau. After several professional positions, including junior designer at Beat Karrer Studio, she joined Designculture AG in 2009 as a part-time product designer.

Tina Stieger graduated in 2006 with a degree in industrial design from FHNW, Gestaltung und Kunst, Aarau. From February 2007 to August 2008 she worked as a Junior Designer at Tjep. In February 2009 she joined Zingg-Lamprecht AG as a part-time stylist.
Pour les Alpes | Neugasse 151 | 8005 Zurich
info@pourlesalpes.ch | www.pourlesalpes.ch

After receiving his high school diploma from Kaiserin-Friedrich-Gymnasium in Bad Homburg in 1986, Lutz Gebhardt (*1960) graduated with a diploma in design. He works as a project manager and teaches at schools of technology and design. His wide scope of expertise is demonstrated in his unique man-machine interfaces.

Mart Hürlimann (*1964) was trained as a machine construction designer and subsequently studied art and industrial design. In 2003 he cooperated with his partners Lutz Gebhardt and Werner Zemp to change the latter's company Zemp+Partner Design into the new quadesign partner ag. Mart Hürlimann is specialized in hardware design.

After completing his training as a cabinet maker, Werner Zemp (*1940) attended the Kunstgewerbeschule Luzern and Ulmer Hochschule für Gestaltung. In the late 1960s, he was drawn to Milano, Chile and England. After his return to Switzerland, he managed Devico Produktdesign. At age 52, he established Zemp+Partner Design.
quadesign partner ag | Untermüli 5 | 6300 Zug
T +41.41.7608670 | F +41.41.7608673 | design@quadesign.ch | www.quadesign.ch

Reto Girsberger (*1968) received his vocational training in design engineering in the defense industry. He received a BA in Science and product design (with honors) from the Art Center College of Design Passadena, CA. Afterwards he worked as Chief Creative Officer and later as Senior Manager for Crealogix AG.
RaceGear | Murstrasse 2 | 8193 Eglisau
T +41.79.3354834 | Reto@racegear.ch | www.racegear.ch

Elena Rendina (*1985) is a photographer, set designer and costume designer. She visited the Liceo Artistico until 2004 and studied Visual Communication/ Photography afterwards at the ECAL, University of Art and Design in Lausanne.
Elena Rendina | Flat1 33A, Temple Street | E2 6QQ London | England
T +44.75.48917920 | info@elenarendina.com | www.elenarendina.com

Richard Amiel (*1961) grew up in New York and received a degree in environmental design from the Parsons School of Design in New York. He worked for several years as a freelancer in Asia and Europe. He has been established his own firm in Switzerland in the year 1992 under the name Rigami Design.
Rigami Design | Sonnenstrasse 1 | 9444 Diepoldsau | T +41.71.7379420
F +41.71.7379421 | info@rigami-design.ch | www.rigami-design.ch

---

Born in 1981 in Switzerland, Adrien Rovero, already the holder of a CFC in interior design and a bachelor's degree in industrial design, received his master's degree in industrial design in 2006 from the Ecole Cantonale d'Art de Lausanne, ECAL, where he is now teaching. He founded the adrien rovero studio in the year of his graduation.
Rovero Adrien Studio | 11, Chemin des roses | 1020 Renens
T +41.21.6343435 | mail@adrienrovero.com | www.adrienrovero.com

---

Silvana Conzelmann (*1955) attended the prep course and graphics curriculum at the Basler Kunstgewerbeschule under Switzerland's top designers, (incl. Eidenbenz, Frutiger, Brun) majoring in illustration and graphic design. Today she manages the design studio Schaffner & Conzelmann, Designersfactory as a co-owner.

Jean Jacques Schaffner (*1954) attended the prep course of the Kunstgewerbeschule Basel followed by vocational training as a sculptor. He also attended the Ecole des Beaux Arts in Paris until 1970. He studied graphic design under Hofmann, Brun, Eidenbenz, Weingart and Frutiger. He is the owner of the Schaffner & Conzelmann agency.
Schaffner & Conzelmann AG designersfactory | Grellingerstrasse 75 | 4052 Basel
T +41.61.2608080 | F +41.61.2608081
info@designersfactory.com | www.designersfactory.com

Lela Scherrer studied fashion design in Zurich and Barcelona. Her work includes assignments for companies like Dries van Noten, Walter van Beirendonck, and ELLE among others. Since 2002 she has been developing women's wear collections and is working on projects with product designers and artists.
Lela Scherrer | Ruetimeyerplatz 5 | 4054 Basel | T +41.61.2712091
info@lelascherrer.com | www.lelascherrer.com

Nicole Benz (*1969) was trained as an elementary teacher, is a musician and attended the prep course and degree program in industrial design at HGK Zurich. She spent a visiting semester at HES Geneva. She is particularly interested in the semantic aspects of design and jewelry.

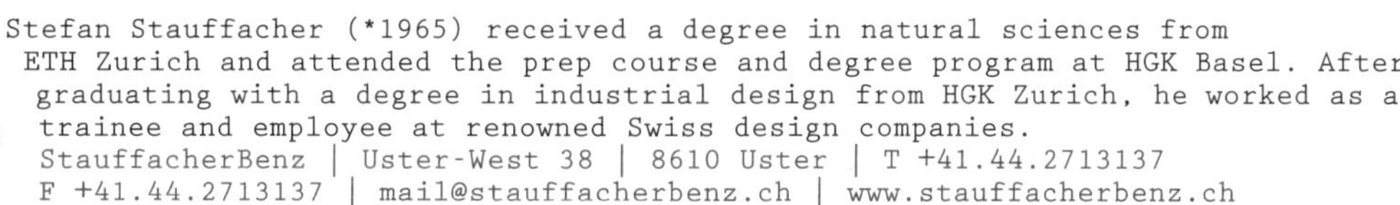

Stefan Stauffacher (*1965) received a degree in natural sciences from ETH Zurich and attended the prep course and degree program at HGK Basel. After graduating with a degree in industrial design from HGK Zurich, he worked as a trainee and employee at renowned Swiss design companies.
StauffacherBenz | Uster-West 38 | 8610 Uster | T +41.44.2713137
F +41.44.2713137 | mail@stauffacherbenz.ch | www.stauffacherbenz.ch

---

Thomas Steuri (*1960) studied education, industrial design and cultural studies in Zurich und Basel. He developed products for many brands such as ABB, Belux, Carl Zeiss Sports Optics, Gardena, Katadyn and established his own company in 2007 in Zurich. He received many awards for his work.
Steuri Industrial Design | Steinwiesstrasse 82 | 8032 Zurich
T +41.43.2685292 | F +41.43.2685292 | mail@thomassteuri.ch | www.thomassteuri.ch

---

Matthias Bischoff holds a degree in product design and is co-owner of the design and production firm "stockwerk3". In addition to associate posts at the Hochschule der Künste in Zurich and Eidgenössische Technische Hochschule ETH Zurich, he works in the area of product design and development at "stockwerk3".

Christof Sigerist holds a degree in product design and is co-owner of the design and production firm "stockwerk3". From the outset he has worked as a product designer with a focus on illumination and lamps. Additionally, he holds various teaching positions, such as at the Hochschule der Künste in Zurich.
stockwerk3 | Balierestrasse 27 | 8500 Frauenfeld
T +41.52.7218181 | F +41.52.7218183 | info@stockwerk3.ch | www.stockwerk3.ch

---

Regula Stüdli works at her studio in St. Gallen. She graduated in the year 2000 with a diploma in fabric design from ZHdk. In 2009 she was nominated for the Swiss Design Award and in 2003 she won the "Die Besten 03 - Silberner Hase" ("The best 03 - Silver Rabbit") award. Since 2001 she has been working as a designer at Jakob Schläpfer.

Regula Stüdli

Benjamin Thut (*1959) is an inventor and designer who has been self-employed since 1992. His work focuses on interior design, trade fair concepts and product design. He attended the Hohere Schule für Gestaltung where he majored in product and interior design.

Thut Möbel | Ackerweg 28 | 5103 Möriken
T +41.62.8931284 | F +41.62.8931110 | info@thut.ch | www.thut.ch

Daniel Irányi studied Industrial Design at the Art Center College of Design Europe. After working as freelancer for companies in Switzerland, South Korea and the United States, he ernrolled to study cultural anthropology before he decided to drop out and co-found Tribecraft, where he is a managing partner.

Jörg Evertz studied mechanical engineering at the RWTH Aachen. He worked at the ETH Zürich as a research assistant focusing on structural analysis and active structures. As co-founder of Tribecraft, he works as a managing partner.

After his vocational training as a toolmaker, Uwe Werner studied mechanical engineer- ing at the Technical University in Chemnitz. He worked at the ETH Zurich as a research assistant in several industry-driven projects before he co-founded Tribecraft, where he is a managing partner.

Tribecraft AG | Binzstrasse 7 | 8045 Zurich
T + 41.44.4854580 | F + 41.44.4854599 | www.tribecraft.ch

Luiza Vogt received her diploma in jewelry and tools design from HFG Pforzheim in 2004. After graduation, she has been working as a jewelry and tool designer at her own workshop in Basel. In addition, she teaches at BBZB in Lucerne since 2007.

Luzia Vogt | Hammerstrasse 178 | 4057 Basel
T +41.61.6833674 | info@luziavogt.ch | www.luziavogt.ch

Thomas Walde graduated in 2006 from the Fachhochschule Nordwestschweiz with a degree in industrial design. After two years of professional experience at 2ndWest, he works today as a research assistant while pursuing his Master's of Arts in design from the Hochschule der Künste in Zurich and he also works as a freelance designer for Postfossil and SEIN.

Postfossil - Thomas Walde | Buchserstrasse 27 | 5000 Aarau | T +41.79.7781831
info@postfossil.ch | www.postfossil.ch

Adrian Weidmann was trained as an industrial mechanic before receiving a degree in industrial design from the Hochschule für Gestaltung und Kunst in Zurich. After his graduation he worked as a junior designer for NOSE Zürich and Industrial Facility and Foster + Partners London.

Adrian Weidmann | Barnet Grove 65 | E1 7BH London | England
M +44.7595.457962 | mail@adrianweidmann.com | www.adrianweidmann.com

Britta Herold (*1973) studied architecture at RWTH Aachen and the University of Sheffield. During her studies she worked for various architecture firms in Aachen, Köln and Bern. After receiving her diploma in 2001 she was assigned with project management for various structural engineering and interior design projects. In 2003 she joined the Hannes Wettstein agency.

Stephan Hürlemann (*1972) studied architecture at ETH Zurich. After graduation, he worked as Chief Content Manager at R.Ø.S.A. Internet Concept and Creation in Zurich. In 2002, he joined the zed. company of Hannes Wettstein as CEO.

Simon Husslein (*1976) graduated in the year 2000 from FH Darmstadt with a degree in industrial design. As a student he already worked as a freelancer for various studios. After graduation he worked closely with Hannes Wettstein at his studio for five years. In 2008 he became a member of the board of management of the Hannes Wettstein studio.

After completing his vocational training as a mechanic, Matthias Weber (*1973) studied jewelry and industrial design at the Hochschule für Gestaltung und Kunst in Zurich. Starting in 1999 he worked as an industrial designer for well-known studios. In 2004 he joined the agency of Hannes Wettstein and in 2008 he became a member of the studio's management.

Studio Hannes Wettstein AG | Seefeldstrasse 303 | 8008 Zurich
T +41.44.4212222 | F +41.44.4212266
info@studiohanneswettstein.com | www.studiohanneswettstein.com

Ramon Zangger (*1953) completed his vocational training in carpentry and interior design in 1977. Until 1981 he participated in several national and international projects while working for Keller & Bachmann. In 1984 he took over the Hans Rechsteiner carpentry and joinery.

R. Zangger-Rechsteiner Möbelwerkstatt | Surtuor 12 | 7503 Samedan T
+41.81.8525495 | F +41.81.8523337
Info@ramonzangger.ch | www.ramonzangger.ch

After graduation in 1998 from the design prep course at the Schule für Gestaltung in Basel, Fabian Zimmerli gained initial work experience in Zurich. In the year 2003 he received his diploma in industrial design from the Hochschule der Künste in Zurich after which he joined Zimmerli Design.

Kurt Zimmerli completed his vocational training as a machinery and constructing draftsman in1966 and attended the Schule für Gestaltung in Basel. Following various practical training periods in Geneva and Zurich, he worked from 1971 to 1985 as a product designer at SIGG AG. In the year 1985 he established his own company, Zimmerli Design.

Zimmerli Design | Dorfstrasse 5 | 8532 Warth
T +41.52.7471848 | F +41.52.7471871
mail@zimmerlidesign.ch | www.zimmerlidesign.ch

Rolf Indermühle (*1978) graduated with a degree in architecture from EPF Lausanne and received a diploma in interior design and scenography from HKG Basel in the year 2005. He was a member of 'les garçons' from 2002-2006 and co-founder of ZMIK in the year 2006.

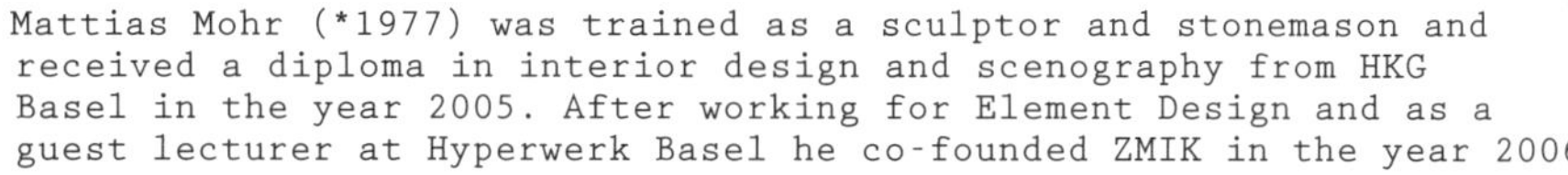

Mattias Mohr (*1977) was trained as a sculptor and stonemason and received a diploma in interior design and scenography from HKG Basel in the year 2005. After working for Element Design and as a guest lecturer at Hyperwerk Basel he co-founded ZMIK in the year 2006.

Magnus Zwyssig (*1974) was trained as a constructional engineering draftsman and gained initial work experience at IRS Architekten. This was followed by a diploma in architecture and scenography from HKG Basel in the year 2005. After working for HHF Architekten, he co-founded ZMIK in the year 2006.

ZMIK | studio for spacial design | Kraftstrasse 5 | 4056 Basel
T +41.61.3212871 | F +41.61.3212893 | kontakt@zmik.ch | www.zmik.ch

Imprint

SWISS DESIGN

The Deutsche Nationalbibliothek lists this publication in the Deutsche Nationalbibliografie; detailed bibliographical data are available on the internet at http://dnb.d-nb.de.

ISBN 978-3-03768-048-3

www.braun-publishing.ch

1st edition 2011

Project coordinator: van Uffelen Editorial office
Editorial staff: Marek Heinel, Sarah Schkölziger
Translation: Cosima Talhouni
Graphic concept and layout: Michaela Prinz

BRAUN